Hygge

The Practical Guide to Incorporating The Secrets of the Danish art of Happiness That can Bring Unlimited Joy into Daily Life

By
Alexandra Jessen

© Copyright 2019 Alexandra Jessen, Hygge

The Practical Guide to Incorporating The Secrets of the Danish art of Happiness That can Bring Unlimited Joy into Daily Life- All rights reserved.

In no way is it legal to reproduce, duplicate, or transmit any part of this document in either electronic means or in printed format. Recording of this publication is strictly prohibited and any storage of this document is not allowed unless with written permission from the author. All rights reserved.

Table of Contents

Introduction 6

What Is Hygge? 7

Hygge Manifesto 11

Hygge of the Mind 16

Hygge and Nature 34

365 Days Hygge 40

Incorporating Hygge as a Lifestyle 57

Hygge and Relationships 88

Hygge Music and Movies 112

Hygge and Food 119

Hygge and Self-Care 134

Conclusion 139

Hygge

As someone who has tried absolutely everything in the pursuit of happiness and the peace we all long for, I realized it can't be found in the latest iPhone or the 100 room mansion, while these things can be amazing and fun, they won't lead to lasting happiness. But, even more than that is all the meaningless 'stuff' we have collected and consumed over the years actually weighs us down and with it drags down our mood and can make us feel heavy. One day, it simply became too much for me and I took a stand, I decided to declutter my house and get rid of anything that didn't serve a purpose or provide me with enjoyment, happiness or joy I decided to get rid of it. This didn't mean I got rid of all my possessions, instead it was the start of a life long journey towards basing my life on what I love and find meaningful.

I will never be someone who lives in a box with 3 possessions to their name, however, I have learned that living in a way that serves you and actually leaves you feeling fulfilled and happy in every moment. No longer am I trying to find myself through objects how I used to. And, what I have decided to do is to share and help as many people live in a way that makes them as happy as they can be. There are no rules to this form of Hygge, everyone is different and that's what makes us human, but please approach all of these works by me as works that are only attempting to help you as much as I can from my own experience and years of research into what makes humans happy and joyful.

It's time we started focusing on what matters, and living life in a way that we love, that is meaningful and that fills us up with fulfillment, and I hope I can help you on your Journey.

Inside this book, I am uncovering the art of the happiest people in the world- Hygge. There must be a reason the Danish are always seen as the happiest bunch in the world and I made it my mission to discover why and then share with you, how you can also become a much happier person, I hope you enjoy!

All the best,

Alexandra

Introduction

Hygge is the most recent lifestyle trend that took the internet by storm. You can see it everywhere, from Instagram to Facebook, which prompt everyone to think "Well, what is hygge? And how do you even pronounce the word?" Or maybe you already know what it is and what values it can bring into your life. Whatever the case, you are reading this because you want to know more about hygge. You want a definitive guide about how to bring it into your life but have been unlucky so far because many other books or guides have been ambiguous at best. If so, then you have come to the right place.

In this book, we will be looking at Hygge, its elements, principles, and fundamentals so you can understand what hygge really is. We will also discuss various implementations of hygge throughout the year, its effects on the mind, and relationship. Most importantly, we will discuss how you can implement it as a lifestyle with the right music, food, and self-care routine. Without further ado, let us get into it.

Alexandra Jessen

What Is Hygge?

Hygge as a lifestyle is hard to explain, and trickier to pronounce. All over the world, hygge (pronounced "hoo-gah") has garnered worldwide popularity. It translates to coziness, but it is a lot more than that. So, what really is hygge?

The word itself is the entirety of the Danish culture. In an essence, hygge means to create a warm atmosphere and savor the simple pleasure in life with good people. What constitutes hygge? The warm glow of the candlelight, cuddling up with your loved one under a soft blanket, gazing out of the window on a snowy Sunday afternoon with a cup of hot chocolate in hand, or sitting around with friends and family, discussing all the big and small, insignificant things in life. That is why the Danes are the happiest bunch in the world, and it is not a big surprise when you think about it. But where did this spirit of hygge come from?

Though Hygge reflects the cozy lifestyle of the Danes, the word itself did not come from the Danish language. It is an old Norwegian word meaning something like "wellbeing" and the word made its first appearance at the end of the 18th century in Danish writing. Since then, the Danes embraced the spirit. Perhaps the best thing about hygge is that you can apply it anywhere, no matter where you live.

Hygge

Denmark is the top three happiest countries of all 155 surveyed countries, and the United State is the eighteenth, according to the World Happiness Report. Denmark's place in the happiness rank is not a coincidence. Their way of life makes them happier, which is the entire spirit of hygge. It is the humble, slow and simple lifestyle. The Danes are obsessed with the use of candles and dim lighting aspects of hygge in particular, but that is not a bad thing.

This obsession comes with the lack of lighting during the cold, harsh winter months from October to March. During this time, darkness is aplenty and everyone gets sick of not seeing the sun. To make matters worse, the Danes also have about 180 days of rain a year, which means they have six months of winter and another six months' worth of rain. Live in Denmark for a year or so and anyone would start to feel quite miserable. To combat the dark and gloomy mood that the weather brings, the Danes turned to hygge.

The first problem is the light, and a fluorescent tube light will not do. They want something that produces soothing light. And so, the Danes carefully select lamps and place them at the perfect locations to illuminate their home just the right way. When the summer months come, you will see many Danes going to the beach where they will spend most of their time basking in the sun, taking in as sunlight as possible. Hygge is a part of the Danes DNA.

Alexandra Jessen

Of course, you do not need to be Danish nor do you need to live in Denmark to practice hygge. Hygge is a feeling, an action, and a mood. In many societies, hygge can be replicated. The idea is to celebrate rituals, cultures,and traditions that involve being close to those you love and care about. It is about not looking upward and be in an endless loop of greed, but being content with what you already have and enjoy the simple things in life. It is about creating the cozy atmosphere that promotes wellbeing.

Hygge does not mean that you must go out and socialize, either. If you are an introvert, you can just stay inside and read a good book by the window. That works just as well. But you should remember that hygge is a thing that happens spontaneously. You cannot plan coziness, but you can create a good condition to cultivate it by arranging your room, spending time with your friends, or meeting someone in a special way.

As you may notice, there are hundreds of hygge guides out there and its popularity is at an all-time high for very good reasons. The main essence of hygge is contentment, which is a feeling of security and safety where we can relax and enjoy the small, simple pleasures of the immediate moments. Hygge is not a demanding lifestyle.

Many lifestyle philosophies that promise a better life force us to commit and deny ourselves the simple pleasures in life. Clean eating or decluttering need us to regularly monitor our own habits, which many people cannot maintain over a long period of time.

Hygge

Alternatively, hygge does not ask us to do anything much. We do not need to give up enjoying the warmth of our espresso in the morning, we do not need to clean our homes if we don't feel like it. It is generous in spirit, without any exercises or diets. Instead, hygge just asks us to loosen up and take things slower. Taking short breaks from the buzz and rush of life and give yourself the pampering that you deserve.

So, why is it so famous? Hygge has made a big impression on the Western world, especially Britain (no surprise there), for a very good reason. When you say hygge, you think of a crackling fire, knitted socks, steaming beverages, the companionship of your friends and family, and a carefree conversation about anything. That is what we all want in a life full of chaos. We want simplicity and love, and that is what hygge provides.

Alexandra Jessen

Hygge Manifesto

There are several questions regarding what counts as hygge. For example, do sweatpants count as hygge? Actually, yes. There is a Danish word for the kinds of pants that you would die rather than wear them in public but they are all that you wear at home binging. Those kinds of pants are called hyggebukser in Danish.

There is actually a word describing things that are hygge-like, "hyggelig", and you may notice that the Danes love to add hygge to other words to describe things. For instance, a hyggekrog is a nook where you can cozy up. This can be a room where you can wrap yourself up in a blanket like a burrito and watch the day pass by, or in your favorite armchair and spend the rest of the day reading a good book. Other than that, here is what is considered to be hygge:

Candles

Any Danish person will tell you that candles are critical when you need to create a hyggelig atmosphere at home. Here's a fun fact: Danes burn thirteen pounds of candle wax a year per capita which is more than any other country in the world according to Wiking. That is an insane amount, but it is worth all the candles. So, turn off all of those fluorescent tube lights and start lighting some candles.

Fireplaces

There are only a few things that make you feel cozier than curling up by the fire with a cup of hot chocolate. You can even decorate your mantel for winter to help you get into the mood better.

Throw Blankets

It can be a heated throw, weighted blanket, or a chunky knit, you need to have something soft to wrap yourself in. Anything that is knitted works like oversized sweaters or thick socks.

Sweets, Comfort Food, and Hot Drinks

To create a cozy vibe, you need to change what you eat as well. Restaurants can deliver the hygge atmosphere like putting candles on tables or installing a fireplace, but you do not need to spend a lot of money on an expensive meal to get those cozy vibes. It is not the point of hygge. It is more about comfort and familiarity.

For the Danes, that can mean pastries, meatballs, and plenty of coffee. In America, you can get yourself a warm drink, spend a lazy Sunday afternoon baking chocolate cake, or dig up your grandmother's chicken pot pie recipe.

You might think that wrapping yourself up in soft fabrics and eating comfort food or sweets should be done in the winter, the Danes have been practicing this concept year around. In the summer, hyggelig activities include picnics, dinner parties in the backyard, bonfires on the beach, or even outdoor movie nights.

Strict Rules

Hygge is about keeping things simple while encouraging people to live a little and say yes when you are offered an extra slice of cake. Looking at the stress-filled years that often divide couples and drain people of their will to live, it is no mystery why Americans are all hyped for hygge.

Good Company

One of the least hygge thing you can do, which happens to be a habit of many people, is starting at their phones all day. Watching television is okay but try to invite your friends or family over to watch movies with you because togetherness is a key part of hygge. Whatever you do, try to be surrounded by those you love and care for. You should always put away devices and spend time genuinely talking to one another.

Staying inside and drinking hot chocolates with a book is hygge, but that is not the entire idea. Another part of it involves going on for long walks even in the cold weather and spending time with your friends and family. Going out brings you closer to nature, its calmness, serenity and give you a better perspective of the world. Nature has healing power.

Minimalism

In a nutshell, hygge is about creating a cozy atmosphere. It is about the mood and vibes than the objects. That means you do not need to buy expensive things to get the cozy vibes. In fact, buying a lot of expensive things is the opposite of hygge. The UK and American style of hygge can be said to be an opportunity for companies to cash in on the hype.

Keeping things simple is the name of the game. Minimalism applies to both the food you eat, the clothes you wear, and the home decorations you put up.

Wholeheartedness

Mindfulness is another element in hygge. It is the idea that we remain in the present moment. It is similar to engaging with your senses, but you also need to enjoy those moments. Hygge is the nonchalant noticing of our immediate surrounding and we engage in all of our senses when we enjoy any given moment, savoring everything that it has to offer. Though simple, it is a lot harder to accomplish.

The basic idea is that you should always seek simple pleasure every day. This is where candles help. Lighting a candle on the dinner table helps bring you back to the present, slow down your fleeting thoughts and giving you the moment of intimacy that you need.

Instead of waking up and rushing out of the house with a slice of toast in your mouth, take the time to brew coffee and enjoy the morning cool from your kitchen window. Instead of saying hi without even looking at each other, make an effort to really connect with your family. No shouting "Hi!" across the room while you are watching TV. They say that it is the little things that count. It takes just a few minutes to ask how each other's day has been. Soon, you will feel that your house becomes warmer and friendlier. It is only natural. A family often bickers among itself and showing that you care will help lift the tension, remind everyone that what a family is really about. Hygge is, after all, a fleeting moment of pause. It is not an escape, but rather the small moments that make life worth living.

Interaction is critical for hygge. Because the sense of belonging is part of hygge, it makes sense to expand your comfort zone to include other people, to feel that we are safe in this small group as we are when alone. The Danes think that getting together is important and they put in the effort to make it happen. Try to have lunch with your colleagues weekly, or make Wednesday night your friends' night. Make those small changes and plan your weekly activity in advance. It may not feel spontaneous, but doing so will help you see who matter to you.

Hygge of the Mind

Hygge only works if your mind is aligned with the environment you are trying to set up. That is the entire point of hygge – making you feel cozy. It all starts with three hygge principles: pleasure, presence, and participation.

A Sensory Experience

We need to engage all our senses as much as possible. Most of the time, we are so preoccupied about work that we overlook the simple things. The simple scent of coffee in the morning, that cool breeze, the soft chatters, and other incredible yet simple moments that happen only occasionally. When we engage in our senses, everything becomes more calming and our emotions and senses enforce them. That is why some people just want to go somewhere far away and lay in the sun all day. Imagine the beautiful beach with the sun on your face, listening to the sound of the waves. Enclosed, secure spaces are essential to hygge and the places that make you feel that you can let your guard down allow you to savor the moment better.

The Danes always have their own hygge hjorne or hygge corners. These corners are all over the house so the Danes can enjoy the warmth of a cozy chair or protect themselves from the elements.

Hygge is a return to the scripts we have inherited. We revisit the places and people that make us feel whole. If your parents used to read you a bedtime story before bed, then cuddling up with your child and read them bedtime stories might bring back some memories of when you were young, making the simple moment more memorable.

Hygge Corner

So, how do you create your own hygge corners?

First, location is crucial. In an ideal situation, you should have a comfortable armchair in an out-of-the-way spot in your house. This is a place where you can read, think, daydream, drink a warm beverage, or take a nap. If you don't have a chair, the corner of the sofa works just fine. Just make the space around it comfortable and cozy.

Next, you will need a fewpieces of furniture. Set up a side table to set a cup within easy reach. At the same time, make sure to have a coaster for your drink so the hot cup of tea or coffee does not ruin the finish on your side tables. For the lighting, consider using a lamp or candles. Twinkling lights are optional, but they add a nice touch. Of course, the corner would not be complete without a fluffy blanket or throw. Make sure that there is plenty of those available in every hygge corners. To keep yourself occupied, have some books and magazines ready. Keep them in a basket or a magazine holder and sort them properly. Let's say, one for those that you have read and another that you haven't.

Other non-essential items include a box of tissues, just in case. If you do read, consider investing in a pair of reading glasses. Touch up space with flowers or a potted plant. Having manicure supplies and hand cream also help if you do wish to pamper yourself. If you wish to eat something sweet, have a candy dish with some chocolates. Just make sure that they are safe from toddlers or your dogs.

If you are not into reading, consider other fun activities like knitting, solving puzzles, or playing solitaire. If you knit or crochet, have a basket with your latest projects nearby. To spice things up, you can play some music from your phone, though some people say that it is more hygienic to use old-fashioned radio or turntable with vinyl records. Again, there is no need to go that far, just use what you have.

Living Space

Consider this an extension of the previous section. If you wish to expand your hygge corner to create a hygge home. So, here are how:

Comfortable Atmosphere

Prioritizing comfort is one of the best ways to create a hygge home. Make sure to stock your living spaces with plenty of warm throw blankets and pillows. Have a comfortable sitting space or nook where you can curl up, read a book, and just unwind. Also, make sure that space is illuminated with soft, natural light.

When you establish a sense of comfort for both yourself and your guests, you are creating a space where people can linger, relax, and enjoy each other's company. Doing this alone sets you up well on your path to living a hygge life.

Color

Colors can influence our mood. They can make us more productive, focused, or comfy. So, you will want to create a calm, relaxing space using neutral tones such as beige, tan, gray, or slate blue. That way, you have a space that is welcoming.

Temperature

Some people are sensitive to temperature. Some are always cold. Some always want the AC on the lowest temperature even if it is snowing outside. Some are both, being too cold in the winter and too hot in the summer. It becomes a challenge to find that sweet spot between hot and cold when heating and cooling are becoming costly. Of course, you can always keep an electric blanket and a few fans handy to regulate the temperature. But if you have a fireplace in your home, light it up. It provides a welcoming warmth during the cold months and gathering around it is a huge part of hygge living, after all.

Enclosed Porch

If possible, you should also invest in an enclosed porch to help regulate temperature. Of course, you should always think very carefully when you want to undergo any form of home improvement. Think of the work that will go into the project and what you can get from it. The same applies to your porch because it is the face of your home. There are a few things you need to consider before deciding.

First is, of course, the weather. If you live in San Antonio, then you should really invest in one. Enclosing your porch allows it to share the same air conditioning with the rest of your home, which is very useful in the summer when it gets blisteringly hot and you just want to sit on your porch with a cold drink but do not want to leave the comfort of your air-conditioned home. The same applies to the colder months. The shared heating will warm up the porch nicely so you can snuggle up with a cup of hot cocoa on your porch. Of course, thanks to the extra space, you should expect to pay extra for both your heating and cooling. Also, you should only heat up or cool down your porch when you need to use it because it is a waste of money and energy otherwise.

Next, you need to look at the upfront cost of installation. Enclosing a porch is cheaper than adding a new room. However, that does not mean that the former is cheap. While the price could be different, expect to pay roughly the same amount as that of a patio installation or something similar. That is why you should not make the decision too hastily. Also, your new enclosed porch does not have as many uses as a new room. So, know what you want your porch enclosed for.

Next, you need to know how will you use it. How often do you think will you use your porch? If you do not know, then do you use it often now? Would you use it more often if it is enclosed? The, what will you use it for? If you want to create a new space to relax in, then you should go ahead and enclose your porch because it works well as a gathering space just like the living room. If you have children, you could use it as a play space. However, if you want to add a bedroom to your house, you might as well go with a new room altogether. Basically, an enclosed porch should have temporary uses. No one wants to talk into your bedroom first when they enter your home, after all. If you want something specialized and permanent, forgo the enclosed porch.

Then, you should look at the law. As with any home improvement project, you need to make sure that you are following the zoning laws in your area. There are actually many factors that go into these regulations such as the end of your property line, whether there are any power or gas lines nearby or even specific rules to your neighborhood. You need approval for your project before you can proceed with it, but you should not stress too much about it because the process usually seems to go off without a hitch.

You should also consider your resale value because an enclosed porch can greatly affect the resale value of your home. This depends on the quality of your porch renovations, of course. A well-done porch will add value to your home, and a bad one will do the opposite. You should not go into a home-improvement project without thinking that you can increase the resale value without investing time, money, and effort into it. If anything, a bad home improvement is worse than no improvement at all.

Finally, think about your yard. A porch is a great addition to your home, but it can take up space in your yard. If your yard is rather tight on space, then you should not invest in an enclosed porch. Of course, it all depends on how important your yard is to you. If you believe that you have more use for an enclosed porch than a yard, then,by all means, go right ahead.

Having an enclosed porch would mean that you can enjoy both the summer and winter without any discomfort. You can watch the world go by from the open space while remaining in the comfort of your own home. Whatever you do, keep the temperature because it is very important when it comes to keeping you cozy.

Homey

You should make your home as comfortable as possible if you want to create a hygge home, then add your own personal touches. How do you make your place more "feeling at home"?

Well, you can use picture frames, art, books, and memorabilia. They all make a big difference.

However, keep in mind that hygge is not about complexity so do not just fill your space with things. Remember that the Nordic homes are minimalist but warm. Using natural materials add a timeless element to your design.

In fact, those who live the hygge life decorate their home with plants to enhance the natural feeling. It creates the feeling of nature, warmth, and comfort, which are perfect for a hygge home. Adding plants also add to the color in your living space, not to mention that it freshens up the place and help to reduce stress. In fact, the benefits of having plants in your living space are well-documented. To keep things as simple as possible, get a few low maintenance potted plants such as bonsai trees, bamboo plants, or succulents. Plants bring about life in the space and it also provides clean air, so it's a win-win.

Candles

Candles are some of the most important things to create a hygge atmosphere. In a hygge home, you need to have them lit all winter long and line them up on the balcony or patio during the warmer months. A candle with tea by the morning and a candle with dinner every evening should be your ritual. The flickering light from the candles add to the warmth of the room and make the atmosphere seem comforting. Lighting is a simple ritual that focuses your senses and allows you to be in the present and being content, after all.

Finding the Positive

The world is a hostile place, and everyone wants to find comfort. Hygge serves as a mean to do that. Make an effort to seek out good news and not the scary headlines. Start a coffee club of writers to share successes, not just moans. Join local initiatives that you once thought that you were too busy for. Find that sense of belonging by connecting with others and yourself so you feel emboldened and embodied.

Mindfulness

As mentioned earlier, hygge is all about being present and "in the moment". This is achievable through the use of candles, but they are only brief. To help you slow down, you also need to understand mindfulness and meditation practices. Thankfully, these things are very simple, which fit in perfectly with the hygge lifestyle.

Meditation

Basically, meditation is a mind-training practice that has many psychological and physiological benefits to those who practice it. It reduces stress, keep anxiety under control, enhance your sense of self-awareness, increases your attention span, prevents memory loss, regulates your emotion, fights addictions, improves sleep, helps relieve pain, and decreases blood pressure. So, you can never go wrong with meditation a while every day. While meditation has many purposes, this section will cover how you can meditate to achieve mindfulness and put you in a relaxed state – a trance if you will.

What You Need

First, you need a place to meditate. This can be your hygge corner if you want but make sure to choose your space wisely. The place should have enough light and open enough to let the fresh air in, not to mention that you need enough space to allow yourself to open up. Now, if you have been working on your hygge corner, then it is perfect because it helps you relax which makes it easier for you to start meditating. Also, make sure that it is quiet so you will not become distracted.

Then, you will need a seat. This can be a chair, a couch, a meditation cushion, or a meditation bench. Since minimalism is a fundamental part of hygge, you do not need to go out of your way to buy a meditation cushion or bench if you do not have it with you. A chair or couch will do just fine. Just make sure that you sit up straight when you meditate, not leaning against anything.

Next, you should get a timer because it is easy to lose track of time when you close your eyes. Since it is built into your phone, you can just use that. Set it to tell you when to stop meditating.

How to Sit

There are literally hundreds of variations of meditation forms both in movies or television. So, it is easy to become overwhelmed and confused about the right way of sitting down and meditate. However, they share some common traits.

Close the eyes fully or keep them partially open. If you can focus on your breathing with your eyes closed, do that. If you feel sleepy with your eyes closed, open your eyes a bit and focus on the nearest object in your sight. Experiment and see what works for you.

For your head, tilt it slightly upward so to open up your body and helps it relax. Plus, it takes pressure off your neck when you lean your head back a bit, not to mention that it helps with your bad neck posture (slumping forward).

For the hands and legs, put them wherever you feel the most comfortable. You can intertwine your fingers, put one palm over other, or just put them on your laps or knees. You can cross your legs, put them in a pretzel-like position, or just put them normally when you sit on a chair.

While there are several types of meditations out there, you should always meditate in a way that allows you to be comfortable while remaining alert. Comfort and alertness should be your top priority. If you are uncomfortable, it will be hard to concentrate. If you are too comfortable, you might fall asleep. Find that perfect balance that allows you to be comfortable but alert at the same time. In the end, the pose, form, or placements of hands and legs are up to you. You choose which one is the best for you, and stick to it.

Meditating

When you have found the perfect meditation place and get into a comfortable position, set the timer. If you are just starting out, we recommend you go for only five minutes of meditation. Start small then work your way up. Meditation might look easy, but it is harder than you think and remaining focused for five minutes straight can be challenging for beginners. When you feel comfortable, bump the number up to ten or even thirty minutes.

Then, start breathing and let your body relax. Focus on the breathing. Here, focus on any aspect of your breathing that works for you. You can focus on how the air enters and exits your nose. You can focus on how the air inflates or deflates your longs. You can focus on the stomach. If you have scented up your home, focus on that. Remember that pacing is important to keep your breathing slow and steady. Take slow, deep breaths, and keep your mind empty.

Keeping your mind empty is a lot easier said than done, though. We all used to think so much that not thinking is foreign for our brain. It is easy to get distracted. Still, do your best to focus all of your attention and mind on the breathing but do not stress yourself out too much if you are not doing well at it. Just continue to focus on doing it. If you do get distracted, gently guide your mind back to your breaths. If you find it hard to focus when you exhale, then it is probably because exhaling is a lot subtler than inhaling. If so, try counting your breaths every time you exhale. From one to five, then back to zero. If you find it hard to focus on your breathing or want to try something a little bit more difficult and different, then there are other alternatives that you could try out. You could try to focus on a certain part of the body at a time. Be aware of how that body part feels. You can even try to work your way up from your feet up to your head during meditation. Alternatively, you can place your attention on the light in the room. You can even switch up your point of focus on a daily basis. One day, you focus on the sounds, and the next day, you can focus on the light.

Additional Tips

There are also a few more things you need to remember when you meditate.

First, if possible, try to include meditation into your morning routine and bedtime routine. That way, you will not forget to do it daily, not to mention that you can use meditation to signal your body to transition from or to a relaxed state in the morning and evening respectively. While you can simply skip meditation and launch yourself into the day full of stressful events, your body might not catch on and you will feel tired, making it hard o focus on your work. At the end of the day, meditation allows your body to relax so you can get a more restful sleep.

If you are a beginner, starting out with guided meditation is a good idea. Basically, it helps beginners and experts alike unlock the key to inner peace easier. However, it is not recommended that you use it every time when you meditate. While helpful in itself, you should learn how to access that place of silence and peace on your own. Otherwise, your own journey is not worthwhile. Of course, that does not mean that you should ditch this meditation altogether. You just need to maintain a healthy balance between the guided meditations and solo meditations. Here, there are four main types of guided meditation. Traditional one gives instructions to guide your meditation process. The guided imagery one will encourage you to use your imaginative power to visualize objects, scenes, or journey. The relaxation oneis just music or natural sounds you can listen to so to relax your entire body. The affirmation meditation is intended to feed yourself positive thoughts.

Also, when you meditate, a lot of things will come up in your mind, both good and bad. Observe them as if they are there to help you and develop positive thinking by seeing everything in a kind, and loving way. While your mind is showing you everything, try to take note of what pops up as they can be the source of your anger, anxiety, or frustration. You will recognize them as they present themselves. While you should just brush them aside during meditation, you should stay with those thoughts for a moment. It can be tricky to remain with them without feeling the negativity, but they can help you pinpoint the source of your sorrow so you can address them later. While you are at it, remember that meditation is more than just to relax. It is a journey of self-discovery. So, when you meditate, be aware of your own thoughts because they can be responsible for your behavior. Observe, but never judge nor criticize yourself. See yourself in a friendly way and give yourself love and try to understand yourself.

If you are just starting to meditate, do not worry if you cannot meditate properly because they get distracted for a few seconds during their sessions. The reality is that there is no way you could meditate perfectly. There will always be flaws. Your mind will wander sometimes. When that happens, just guide it back to your breathing. You will get better at it eventually. Many beginners often fail because they cannot commit to meditation. They tried it once or twice, but then give up and say that meditation does not help them at all. In fact, it does, but it just takes time and efforts. Try your best to develop a habit of meditation on a daily basis, and you will soon notice the difference.

Also, after your meditation session, don't forget to smile. Meditation is also a process of giving yourself the attention you need and deserve. Smiling develops positive thinking as well. Be thankful for yourself that you allow yourself some quality time to meditate. Give yourself a pat on the shoulder. Everyone needs some self-love, and this is one of the ways to feed yourself that love.

Common Mistakes

There are many ways to meditate, that much is true. Some aspects of meditation can be modified to fit your own preferences, although many people pay a little too much attention to detail. The most common mistakes people make when they are meditating is the way that they think.

First, never judge your own experience. When you meditate, the goal is to keep your breathing steady and your head clear. Meditation is meant to give your head a break, the silence it deserves. At the same time, it is also the practice of patience and gratitude. We already discussed the fact that you need to keep your mind and heart at peace when you meditate, and beginners tend to worry that they are meditating incorrectly. Instead of worrying, stop and focus on the fact that you are practicing meditation. Focus on yourself and the stillness of emotions.

A quick google search will show that there are many "meditation" necessities that you should buy in order to attain complete mindfulness. That is not true. You do not need them to meditate. It is all about inner peace and external objects are irrelevant. Minimalism is part of hygge, after all. Still, if some of them help, then you can keep some of them around. Just try to keep them to a minimum. Keep the ones that help you focus and relax.

Another problem with the modern world is the fact that we love to add all the bells and whistles to just about anything. Now, you can find hundreds of meditation techniques that have modern twists on the ancient practices. While science has contributed to these modern variations, it is worth noting that they may lack the spiritual experience. Traditional meditation techniques have been developed and have thousands of years of experience in spiritual growth, and that makes them a better choice for serious practitioners. Modern meditation techniques can be fun to try out, but you should stick to the traditional ones.Still, we recommend you start with guided meditations first because it is a lot easier for you to develop a habit of meditating. These kinds of meditations help you unlock the key to inner peace easier. But you should not rely on it every time you meditate. It is indeed helpful, but you need to learn how to access that place of silence and peace on your own. Otherwise, your journey is not worthwhile. Start with guided meditation and then transition slowly to solo meditations.

After meditating for a while, you will start to feel that meditating is boring. Even worse, you might start to feel that it is becoming a chore. By then, you might not want to meditate or even become more stressed about it. How do you avoid this problem? Simple. You can mix things up to keep it interesting. Consider meditating with your eyes open or with soothing ambient music once in a while if you haven't already. If you feel adventurous, try meditating when you are working. All you need to do is keep your head clear and take deep and constant breaths. You do not even need to sit down in a meditating position to start meditating. Just make sure that you are comfortable with the environment before you start.

Hygge and Nature

Because Hygge is a sensory-driven experience, there are many ways to bring it into your life. One way to do that is having items made out of wood. If you have ever been in a Danish home, you will notice that a lot of things are made out of wood. The Danes have wooden floors, tables, and bookshelves. Even children's toys are made out of wood. It might look like the Danes are time travelers, having such antique-looking things in their home, but wood make you feel close to nature. It is simple and natural. You do not need to go outside to be with nature. You can bring it into your hygge home. Imagine how soothing it is to run your finger across a wooden cabinet, or taking in the smell of a wood burning stove or a fireplace, or the creak of a wooden floorboard.

Still, having wooden furniture is not enough for the Danes. They need to bring in the entire forest inside their home, so you might see leaves, twigs, nuts, sheepskin, cowhide, among many other things. Basically, the place looks like a bird's nest. Think of how a Viking squirrel furnish a living room and you have a pretty good idea how the Danes decorate their homes.

In addition to that, nature can also be brought inside through the use of natural light and window space. That is why you should have your hygge corner close to the window (more on that later). In fact, many things hygge involve reading a book near a window and listening to the wind. Having that small element of nature allows you to remain present and appreciate the warmth and joy of being indoors, even if you are practicing hygge indoors.

Still, some people do not like to spend a lot of time indoors. That is fine. It is actually possible to bring hygge with you outside. For the Danes, the time from fall to summer will be spent indoors because of the harsh cold. But in the summer, they are out and about, soaking in as much sun as possible. During those months, they take hygge with them while they go boating, camping, staying in cabins, fishing, picnicking, seeing a movie playing outdoors, and watching meteor showers. Every activities have their own purpose and the Danes strive to be in a place where they can appreciate the simpler things and have quality conversations with those you love.

Of course, there is absolutely no reason to go out and spend thousands of dollars buying quality wooden furniture if you want to experience hygge. This is what this section going to discuss. We will give you some ideas to connect with nature, both indoors and outdoors.

Indoors Ideas

These ideas involve activities that are inside your home, involving areas in your property, or in your work area.

Let Nature In

Start by freshening up your own home. Open those windows, blinds, curtains, and doors (if applicable) to allow the sunlight and natural air to flow into your home to produce a relaxing and natural atmosphere.

Stargaze

Stargazing is a fun and nostalgic way to admire the universe and all of its miracles. Looking at the stars remind us that our lives here on Earth are only a single grain of sand on the beach, and there are millions of worlds out there full of possibilities beyond our wildest imaginations. You can watch the stars from the window, your porch, or in the backyard.

Gardening

This is an activity that directly exposes you to the work of nature, and allow you to nurture life with your hands. As you watch your plant grow, you will realize that gardening is a fascinating experience. You do not need to grow sophisticated plants. Many of plants are easy to maintain, and most of them are edible. You can even grow them indoors. If you decide to grow flowers, you can bring those inside your home as well.

Taking Breaks

Sometimes, all you need to do is to pause for a moment, stand up, go to the window and gaze outside. That way, your eyes can rest. Look at something green. Better yet, go outside and sit on the grass and do nothing. Just connect with the earth.

Speaking of taking breaks, you can also enjoy your cup of tea or coffee break outside. Just go out of the door, and enjoy the stillness. Savor every single sip and soak in the sun and the fresh air.

Reading

Instead of reading inside, go outside and read. Sit on the grass or on the patio and soak in the sun while you read.

Scents

You can bring the smell of nature indoor by wearing an earthy scented perfume or using essential oil. You can also put up diffusers to chunk out the smell of nature as well. We will talk about scents later in the book.

Meditate

Again, instead of meditating inside your home, you can do it on the grass without your mat. Allow yourself to meditate in the sun barefoot and let the grass message you while you meditate. You can also practice yoga this way. More on meditation later.

Outdoors Ideas

These ideas involve going outside beyond your property, and there are many more possibilities than indoors ideas.

Going Barefoot

Make a conscious effort to walk barefoot on the grass or along the beach. Focus on how rejuvenating it is to be connected with nature through your feet and enjoy the grounded sensation that comes along with it.

Speaking of going to the beach, you should also visit the nearby lake or any body of water. Think of it this way. You are visiting the source of life on this planet, and there is something mesmerizing about watching the still calmness of the lake, or watching the rapid flow of the river that also soothes your ears. Take the time and just sit and watch the water.

Walking

While we are on the subject of walking, you should try making an effort to park a distance away from your destination. That way, you give yourself the opportunity to walk and enjoy everything along the way. So, examine the trees, clouds, grass, birds, air, and everything you come across along the way. Also, focus on your senses. What can you smell, hear, and feel?

Speaking of walking, you should try exploring the local area as well. Some people rely on Google Map too much to help them navigate. Most of the time, they will only know one way or two to get to their destination. So, while you are out walking, try exploring. Look around and familiarize yourself with the place.

Exercising

Just like practicing meditation, you can also try exercising outside. Go for a run at the park, or just around the block. Whatever suits you. While you are at it, take in as much fresh air as possible.

365 Days Hygge

Hygge is perfect during the cold months, but you do not have to limit getting your dose of cozy vibes until the snow comes about. Being hygge is more than just getting cozy and feeling good about it. Practicing it year-round supports your mental and emotional wellbeing as well. Here are some ways on how to embrace hygge throughout the entire year:

Simple Rituals

We mentioned earlier that a key element of hygge is simplicity. The best way to start practicing hygge year-round is by working with your daily routine. Think of the time when you feel joy or frustrated. Think of your habits that no longer work for you and then simplify your tasks. For instance, if your morning routine involves rushing out the door to grab coffee or tea, drinking it and eating a slice of toast on the way to work, leaving you stressed, groggy rather than refreshed, then you should reconsider your morning routine. Consider going to bed a bit early so you have enough time to wake up early. That way, you can brew yourself a lovely cup of coffee and enjoy it with the classic bacon and egg. Sometimes, you might just need to slow down and take a deep breath to collect your thoughts before you head out. It all depends on you. Experiment to see what works.

You know when you found the right daily routines when you feel that they are effortless and involve being "in the moment" for the simple satisfying things. If something is forced or rushed, ask why. Then think creatively about how to alter your routine so they nourish you and light up your mood. Being too busy to do anything is not an excuse.

The Five Senses

Creating the right environment is crucial for hygge. Try to create a comfortable and pleasant space where there is no annoyances or distractions. Break everything down into what you can feel, taste, smell, hear, and see. Use these are guides to help determine what help you to be in the moment.

Certain things may work for you all year, but certain things can change from season to season. For example, a bubble bath lit by candles or a glass of wine and a conversation with an old friend can last all year, but decorating your living space with freshly cut flowers from your local flower might only be viable during spring. During the cold months, you might find hygge in the beautiful scent of cinnamon and orange peels simmering on the stove.

Lazing on a hammock with spa water or popsicle, letting the warm breeze caress your body might be a good picture of hygge. A spring equivalent could be a picnic on a blanket spread across the lush green grass, surrounded by beautiful, colorful flowers. What is hygge to you is very personalized, so experiment.

Hygge

Think of a scene or sensation that allow you to loosen up and luxuriate before you turn it into a reality in whatever way makes you feel cozy.

Food

Hygge is incomplete without food. Of course, meals are the perfect time to practice hygge because you can fully savor the dish that nourishes both your souls and your body.Moreover, food provokes memory, nostalgia, making the moment even more enjoyable. That is why you always think back to your mother's cooking when you eat something that tastes like what she would cook for you. Maybe there is a spice that makes you think of home or of your host family's exotic home-cooked cuisine when you studied abroad. Experience recreation with certain dishes never fails to bring you the warm and fuzzy feelings when you remember those beautiful moments. Want to recreate those moments? Go dig out your grandmother's recipe for roasted chicken when you miss your family, or just whip up your mother's special noodle soup.

In terms of stimulating senses, food can satisfy multiple senses. Food goes beyond taste. Imagine how good the smell of freshly baked brownies is, or the sight of a colorful, pretty salad. Eating soup, though simple and insignificant, can be very comforting. Stop eating just to stop being hungry. Start eating to nourish your soul. While we are on the topic of eating, remember to savor every bite. Many people would just wolf down their food so they can continue working again. This is not hygge. Instead, take your time to eat, even if it takes an hour. It is found that people would eat less if they eat slowly. This is because the body has time to register the food coming into the stomach, and tell you when it feels full properly. If you eat too fast, you are already overeating by the time you feel full. Besides, you can remain grounded, in the moment, by savoring each and every bite of your favorite food. Take the time and fully enjoy what you put into your mouth.

Springtime

Hygge is often associated with the cold weather. Hot cocoa, snuggly blankets, roaring fire in the fireplace are the things that come to mind when you say "hygge" or "coziness". However, there are several ways you can bring the spirit of hygge to spring.

Porch Time

As the name suggests, this is the time for you to hang out at the porch. After a bitter winter, get out there when it gets warm enough. It can be in the afternoon, but soon enough you can have your porch time any hour of the day.

In the morning, consider making a cup of delectable Earl Grey and bring it to the porch and enjoy the birdsong and the sunrise. Just take it all in.

In the afternoon, hot tea works just fine but switch to iced coffee if the weather gets too warm. Using incense might help calm your mind while you read or listen to music.

In the evening, line up the porch with candles and incense. If possible, enjoy your dinner with some romantic music and wine. Alternatively, you can also have dinner on the patio when it is warm enough to start grilling. Decorate the space with hanging plants, wind chimes and have a nice table and chairs set up for guests. Imagine having a few friends over for grilled burgers, margaritas, conversation,and music. Isn't that lovely?

Other Activities

The idea of laying on your back in your chairs and just gaze silently at the stars and talking about all the things that are on your mind is a good way to spend your evening. You don't have to talk all the time. Silence is just as good. While you're at it, put on some music.

Going for a walk in the evening is also a good idea. Take your dog out or go with your loved one. Picnics are also a great way to enjoy the spirit of hygge during spring. Pack a basket with food and enjoy a meal with your family at the nearby park.

If you have enough room in the backyard, investing in a fire pit is a great idea. Candles and fireplace are hygge. But a large roaring fire is even more hyggelig. It is mesmerizing about watching a fire dance, and you can spend the evening with your friends and family, talking about anything.

You may be used to drink a cup of tea during the winter, but as spring comes around, it might be time to drink something cooler. A seasonal cocktail, Earl Grey Martini, or other refreshing cool drinks work.

Start planting flowers, herbs, and vegetables. The act of nurturing life with undivided attention. If you grow flowers, you can have fresh flowers in your house to decorate the space. There is no better time to decorate your home with flowers than spring. If not, you can buy them relatively cheap from the local florist. Make sure to change the water and trim the ends regularly to keep the flowers going as long as possible.

Another great idea would be tidying up your room. Winter is miserable and spring is the time to start anew. You do not need to go all in with this. Just make sure to organize things and lighten up the space with bright colors. Of course, cuddling up with your pets or loved one on a lazy Sunday afternoon binging is not a bad idea, either.

Summertime

When the weather gets warmer and warmer, it is time to switch up again. Think of all your favorite moments for the warm weather like picnics, bike rides, farmers markets, outdoor concerts, etc. Here are some tips to bring hygge into the summer.

Dine Outside

Pretty straightforward. This idea involves going out with your friends or those who love for a picnic or a lovely dinner in the backyard. Just like spring, pack the basket with your favorite food and bring some cool drinks like chilled wine. You can display your food on wooden boards and bowls to display the food and drink from glass rather than plastic cups and plates. It takes more effort but it is worth the effort because they are more natural than plastic, making the moment even more memorable and sweeter. It takes efforts to help people slow down and enjoy the moment. It is also a good idea to set up summer flowers nearby. Combine that with beautiful clear glass candle holders, soft candle lights, and homemade food, and you have a beautiful evening.

Spend Time With Nature

The Danes are known to get out as much as possible during the summer because this is the time to get as much sunlight and warmth as possible. The summer season is short, but the temperatures are perfect. So, get plenty of hikes, bikes, and other outdoor activities. Consider playing volleyball at the beach in the afternoon and sitting around a fire in the evening. Spend time out in the backyard with the fireflies. Spending time in nature makes you feel content and calm, so go out there and be with nature. Better yet, call some friends so you can spend some quality time together.

Alexandra Jessen

Spicing Up

When the weather gets warmer, it is time to put away the thick blankets and bring out the summer cotton blankets. Let your creative mind play a part and use bright, summery color to spice up your home. Blue, pink, and yellows are the best. Bringing in colors is not limited to the color of pillows or blankets. Take advantage of the fruits and flowers. Just like spring, change the colors in your home for a fresh feeling in your home. Try to have a bouquet of summer blooms in your house. Consider buying sunflowers, fresh greens,and wildflowers. Having one on the kitchen table, one in the living room and one in the bedroom is a good start. You can buy fruits and flowers cheap from the local vendor.

Autumn

Autumn or fall is the season when things start to get colder again, so it is time to break out the wintry things and have them on standby. In terms of redecorating your home, go for darker colors. Grey and dark orange work, but make sure to not go overboard. Grey blanket and orange pillows work. Candles are, again, important especially during this time of the year. Here are some activities for the autumn.

Activities

October is the best month to start planting tulips, which will bloom in spring so you have fresh flowers for the next year. This is a life-nurturing activity you can do during fall.

A large pot of chili and some homemade cornbread are the entire essence of fall. Both vegetarian or meaty chili work and there is no better excuse to invite over a few friends to enjoy a hearty meal beside the fireplace. Speaking of a fireplace, cooking a meal in your fireplace is even more wonderful. To combat the cold weather, you can make any night of the week a soup night. Couple that with a delicious salad and a loaf of bread and you have a meal that many people will appreciate.

Speaking of food, you can get closer to nature during autumn by going apple picking. Go with a few friends and then plan to make a meal with apples. Apple pies, cider, apple sauce, and baked apples are something you should definitely try. Alternatively, try pumpkin dishes like pumpkin bread. Carving up a pumpkin and creating backed goodies signal the start of the beautiful season.

Looking for some other hobbies? You can take up knitting or crocheting. Start cozying up in your hygge corner (more on that later) and create something beautiful. Maybe knit yourself a blanket or a sweater for the upcoming winter. Do whatever relaxes you is a great way to spend your evening.

Alexandra Jessen

    If you want an activity that involves going out, in addition to going out picking apples, going out camping is a good idea. The campgrounds that were once crowded should be quite vacant at this point so you can enjoy the state parks without the summer traffic. Bring your friends or family along to enjoy this soothing stillness. Plus, you might be able to catch a glimpse of migrating birds. Spending the afternoon bird watching is mesmerizing. Or if being on the move is more of your style, consider cycling around.

Winter

This is the perfect time to practice hygge. This is the perfect time to get warm and cozy in your own home as the snow cover the world like a blanket. So, how do you bring hygge into this season?

Fire

Of course, it is a must for a true hygge experience. If you have a fireplace, put it to good use. If you do not have a fireplace or cannot use it, line up candles instead or build a campfire outside. If you want to use candles, remember that there can never be enough candles. The more you have, the better. When it is dark outside, you will see the magical atmosphere these candles create. They calm you down and put you at ease immediately and the meal you have will feel more memorable.

Hot Drinks

To keep yourself warm, have a mug of hot drinks ready. Hot apple cider with a cinnamon stick or mulled spiced wine, hot chocolate with whipped cream, or tea are perfect. Throughout the winter months, make sure to have plenty of hot drinks ready. If you go with tea, why not try out green tea in the morning, Earl Grey or black throughout the day, and mint in the evening.

Warm Socks

It sucks to feel that you are wearing blocks of ice on your feet. Keep your feet warm is essential for a genuine hygge environment. Wool socks work the best. If you can, splurge on a quality pair and it will make a world of difference, not to mention that they last a very long time. You can also wear hand-knitted leg warmer and other things you've knitted during the autumn.

Good Books

While you can always pick up reading in any other season, you should actually spend those time going outside in the sun. When winter rolls around, you will be spending a lot of time inside so this is a good time to pick up a good book. You can have a cozy evening by the candles or fireplace on your armchair, with your feet propped up by a footstool, with a cup of hot cocoa, reading your favorite book. Does it sound lovely?

Soup

Nothing says hygge louder than a pot of soup simmering on the stove on a Saturday afternoon. If you do not know where to start, cook up a pot of bean, minestrone, or curried lentil soup. Eventually, the whole house will be filled with delectable steam and aroma.

Blankets and Flannel Shirts

If you take a look on Instagram, many of hygge scenes involve blankets. Investing in a quality blanket is a must. You can wrap it around yourself while you enjoy your hot cacao close to the fireplace or cuddle up with your pet or loved one under it. Flannel shirts also add to the mood.

Outdoor

While going outside during winter seems counterintuitive, but you still need to get close to nature. Going on long hikes through the forest, skiing, or ice skating are some activities you should include in your planner. You will feel satisfied, energized, and replete with nature. Getting active once in a while helps you relax. Plus, the fireplace and warmth will be all the more satisfying.

Relax

If you have been busy throughout the entire year, it is time to slow down, and winter is the best time to do so. You cannot have hygge without allowing yourself the time to be. Clear your calendar of obligations. Give yourself the time to hibernate for a few months. Take it as a time to recharge yourself, to catch up on your missed sleep and reading. Take the time to connect with family.

Alexandra Jessen

Starting Fires

Now, the skill of fire-starting is almost taken for granted by those who have lived with fireplaces or did not experience the use of gas to light anything on fire. Unfortunately, not many people are taught the skill that sparked the first-ever technological invention of humanity: fire. Using gas to start a fire is the quickest way, true. At the same time, it is a rather expensive and unnatural way to start a fire. If you struggle to get the fireplace going, then the hygge atmosphere would be ruined by your frustration and you might not want to start the fire again, which takes away a significant portion of the Danish lifestyle. So, here is how you start a fire without investing a ton of cash on starter logs or hours to get the fireplace going.

First, you need to know that there are two ways to lay out the wood. The first is the teepee method, in which you put the logs standing on their ends, leaning against one another to form a, you guessed it, teepee or a cone. The second method is the log house method in which you lay down logs the way they do to build a log cabin. Of course, you can just lay everything down haphazardly, but the fire will not burn as efficiently. Still, we will go for a combination of the two methods. Start by putting down medium-sized logs side by side, leaving a gap about two inches wide and stuff it with newspaper. Then, build a teepee on top of the logs with more newspaper surrounded by a pyramid of kindling. That way, there is enough space for air to come through and a base that will burn so the fire can get going as the teepee burns down.

Of course, before you start building your stacks of woods, make sure that they are actually dry first. Always burn the lightest logs first and try to get the ones with all that jagged edges. Those logs have a larger surface area for the fire to catch on. If all of your logs do not have edges, you can grab an ax or something to cut diagonally into the log to create that jagged edges along the side of the logs. For the kindling, it should be split in various sizes so they burn at a different speed.Also, you should use newspaper as your kindling, but not the glossy ones. The only issue now is which method is the best to burn the newspaper. This is a widely disputed topic. Some say twisting, some say ripping strips, but scrunching seems to be the best way to go about this.

Now that you have your fireplace set up, make sure to watch the fire constantly. Fires eat up wood faster than you think and they need to be fed a lot in the early stage, which will take some time. Spending about fifteen minutes should be enough as you keep adding pieces of kindling or twigs. Just make sure to grab bigger and bigger pieces to add to the fire. Eventually, the fire will be big enough to start eating up small logs. Use your instinct and find that sweet spot between suffocating the fire and feeding the fire. This can be a bit frustrating, but you will get better at it with time. Plus, spending fifteen minutes now will save you a lot of frustration in the future.

Alexandra Jessen

Always keep the airflow in mind as you work the fire. There should be enough for it to go through the teepee, or else the fire will splutter and die. While you can blow some air to revive the fire, it is not the way to keep the fire going. Blowing air should only be used to revive or rearrange wood if you need to.

Eventually, as the fire gets bigger, you will be able to lean large logs against each other to form a roof over the base. Alternatively, you can also lay them in perpendicular to the bottom logs depending on how well-established the fire is, although this method would mean risking suffocating the fire if it is not large enough.

You need to keep watching the fire until there is a good coat of white coals on the bottom and the fire has been going for quite a while.

When it comes to building campfires or bonfires, you need to first understand the law of how fire burn. You might be familiar with how bonfires are set up, but probably have no idea why. The best way to build a bonfire is by having the width of the base roughly the same to its height. Bejan researched how fires work back in 1996 and he published his findings (go, science!). Without getting into the scientific details, the wide but short fire gets hotter as the fire gets taller because of the increased airflow at the top. The skinny but tall fire gets hotter as the fire gets shorter because of the sheer volume of wood at the bottom. So, build a bonfire that balance the two (width and height) for the optimal heat production.

Hygge

    It's also worth mentioning that, if you are out camping and need kindling, use dead sticks because they are dry. Live branches are actually wet, which do not help the fire at all. So, choose dead sticks that snap easily in your hands.

Alexandra Jessen

Incorporating Hygge as a Lifestyle

People see hygge as a means to promote a feeling of contentment, which is why so many people are interested in the concept. It is a way to create more happiness, friendliness, and wellbeing in everyday life. Hygge is about having a nice time, indulgence, and not denying or punishing yourself for anything. You are just being kinder to yourself and to your companions. Here are some ways you can incorporate hygge into your life.

Lighting

Any Danish person will tell you that the best way to create a hyggelig atmosphere is using candles. Danes go through candles like hotcakes. In fact, they use so many candles that they have the term "lyselukker" meaning "someone who puts out candles" to address those who is a spoilsport.

Fortunately, you do not need to spend a fortune on candles even though you will be burning through a lot of them. IKEA, Bed Bath & Beyond, Amazon, Target, and other stores have large bags of about 100 tea lights for under $15. Just make sure to practice basic fire safety by not placing candles near anything that is flammable, far out of reach of your pets and children. Most importantly, never leave a burning candle unattended. It is hygge to have candles, but it not hygge when your house is the candle.

Another lighting method you should consider is a fireplace. If a candle is cozy, then a fire is a lot cozier. It feels more immersive to watch the flame dance than feeling the warmth from the electric bulbs and central heating. During the summer season, you and your friends or family can gather around a campfire in an outdoor fire pit. Even when cooking a meal over a barbecue grill allows you to watch the flame dances and you can toast a few marshmallows.

During the winter months, if you do not have a fireplace, get creative! Stream a video of a crackling fire on your TV, which is close enough. You will not feel the heat, but you can still watch the flames and hear the logs pop. A quick google search on YouTube is all it takes.

Comfy

You will not feel cozy in your business suit. Change into something comfortable to get hygge. Heavy sweaters and knitted socks work best during the winter season because they keep you warm and they are so soft.

Moving About

While the Danes have six months of winter and six months of rain, you might think that they will only go out when the sun shines. In reality, they love to go for long walks in all kinds of weather. Walking is hyggelig in itself when you have friends with you. It is a chance for you to talk to them and enjoy each other's company without costing a penny. But you can go on walks on your own or with your dog if you want to clear your mind from all the buzz of your work.

Biking

In addition, bicycles are also very popular in Denmark. According to the nation's official website, its capital city of Copenhagen is known for its cycling culture and it is recognized as the first official bike city in the world. Because bikes move slower than cars, you get the time to enjoy the scenery which makes them hygge. If you have a bike, consider cycling to work. Numerous studies have proven that those who bike to work are both happier and healthier than those who drive. IF you don't have a bike, you do not need to buy an expensive one either. A secondhand one works just fine. Craigslist and eBay often have simple bikes in good condition for less than $100. If your city has one, consider joining a bike sharing program to cut the cost further.

According to the Brookings Institution, 85% of Americans drive to work alone or in carpools. Only 5.1% use public transit, 2.7% walk, and 0.6% bike. In larger cities, walking and transit are more popular but biking is still left in the dist. Of course, car commuting remains the most favorite means of transportation, making up more than three-quarters of all trips even in major metro areas with long commute times.

Hygge

While the number of cyclists is low even though it is the most convenient and eco-friendly means of transportation, cycling is not a viable option for millions of American workers in areas with low population density and dispersed employment in exurban belts around major U.S. cities. After all, who would want to cycle forty miles every day to work?

According to the U.S. Census, the average commute time for Americans is 25.4 minutes although the Washington Post said more than two million Americans commute longer than 50 miles and about 1.7 million take longer than 90 minutes.

Thankfully, millions of American workers live in large, dense cities or smaller communities or suburbs where they are close to work. If you are one of those lucky people, biking to work regularly is a very viable option.

If you plan to commute regularly by bike, you will need to have certain equipment and clothing can help better your experience.

The first and most important thing to consider is location. If you live somewhere with a wet four-season climate, you need more equipment and clothing compared to those who live in drier, milder places. Other than that, here are a few things you need before you commit to cycling. If you invest in all of these items, you can expect to pay between $350 to $5,000 depending on the brand and quality.

Bike

This is where most of your money will go into. If your current bike is old or unreliable for long-distance, time-sensitive travel, you should buy a new bike. Here, you have two options depending on the nature of your route. If the way to work is all smooth without going offroad, a road bike will do just fine. However, if you want to use your bike recreationally on rough terrain, consider buying a hybrid or mountain bike. Hybrid bikes have thicker tires that have better traction, not to mention that they have supple frames than road bikes, making them an ideal option on rougher terrain. Still, they are not as versatile as mountain bikes.

But it is not exactly hygge to spend thousands of dollars on a bike with all the bells and whistles, is it? If you wish to minimize your upfront investment without compromising the quality, try to find well-made secondhand bikes at the local bike shop. Alternatively, look it up at eBay for a highly rated local reseller. If you feel lucky, look for one on Craigslist. It goes without saying that you should always inspect the product before paying for it. The same applies if you buy used bikes. They should be in a good enough shape to take you to and from work on a regular basis.

A new road bike will cost you between $200 to $5,000 and a secondhand road bike costs you almost half of that price. New and used hybrid and mountain bikes.

Helmet

While helmets are not required by law in your area, wearing one never hurts. The price is between $20 to more than $100. Speaking of protection, you need more than a helmet. In cold or wet condition, cycling can be dangerous so you need to protect your head. A scarf or turtleneck during chilly days works just fine. However, during cold or rainy days, put on a waterproof face mask or cowl. Of course, you also need to protect your eyes, especially when the weather is not optimal. Sunglasses for bright days and sky googles during cold, rainy or snowy days.

New Tires and Tubes

Starting with fresh tires and tubes means that you will not have to worry about the risk of prior wear and tear even if you don't buy a new bike. It is always wise to start your commuting career off on the right foot, after all. Tires are different based on the type and model of the bike but expect to spend between $10 to more than $400. The tube will cost you between $4 to more than $20.

That said, while you are cycling, expect to run into troubles. Rocks, glass, nails, and other types of sharp debris can puncture your tire and ruin your day. Spare tubes are cheap, take only a small space, and changing one is straightforward. You can ask someone at your local bike shop to demonstrate or find an online tutorial.

Pump

Your Bike will lose air pressure, so carrying a bike pump will ensure that you never have to ride on a half-flat tube that damages your wheel. If you want to travel light, consider carrying a pocket pump that compresses air into a narrow cylinder. A pocket pump should run better $7 to $40. If you want a powerful pump pat home, a large standing pump gives more power than a pocket pump and it costs between $10 to $100. Just make sure that the pump fits the tire nozzle.

Headlights and Taillights

If you work full-time, low-light conditions will be inevitable. You will need some headlights and taillights on your bike, and they are required in almost all jurisdictions. It is never a good idea to ride down a darkened street without anything to warn drivers of your presence. Your headlight should be bright enough to light the roadway a few seconds ahead of your bike, but the taillight can be dimmer because it is meant to alert approaching drivers. Buying both the headlight and taillight is usually more cost-effective than buying separately. Expect to spend between $10 to more than $100.

Racks, Panniers, Basket

A setup with a rack and a pannier allows you to carry spare bike equipment, work items, and even clothing on the bike frame.

The rack, which is the thick wire platform that goes over the bike's back wheel can even carry another person. Panniers are basically saddlebags that attach to one or both sides. The rack costs between $20 to $80 whereas the pannier cost between $30 to more than $110. If you plan to get an integrated solution, consider a bike with a spacious cargo like the Spicy Curry from Yuba Bikes. Their pedal-assist electric bike options are both helpful for those who have hilly or long commutes while still giving the cyclist a great workout.

Optional Items

If you do not want to weigh down the back or front of your bike, consider investing in a canvas backpack instead of racks and panniers. However, if your load is too heavy, you run the risk of straining your back so get an adjustable backpack that fits your back.

During the rainy season, muds will be your worst enemy. Nothing ruins your day more than being soaking wet and having mud stick to your bike. So, invest in bike fenders. They attach to your front and back wheels to capture the splash, protecting your ride from mud, dirt, and water. They can be a life-saver. Speaking of getting wet, you should invest in waterproof clothing as well. Though a bit expensive, they can make your travel in the rain much more pleasant. For example, water-wicking socks can reduce discomfort if your boots or shoes are not waterproof. Invest in waterproof athletic pants or sky pants, along with a windbreaker or raincoat.

To protect your bike, consider investing in locks unless you can bring your bike into your office. Get a solid metal U-lock because it is a lot harder to pick or cut than flexible cord lock.

Finally, make sure to have a water bottle handy. Even on short bike commutes, you need to remain hydrated. Invest in a bottle holder and a good plastic or metal water bottle is always a better option compared to disposable bottled water.

Food

It is much more hyggelig to cook your meals at home than eating out. It's even better if you share the meal with someone you care about. If you want to make your dinner as hygge as possible, focus on comfort food rather than exotic cuisine. Cooking up food using fresh and natural ingredients are good, but there is no need for a fancy presentation. If you want to, you can whip up popular Danish dishes like pancakes, and meatballs. However, you can eat whatever feels most comforting to you. If you do wish to eat with your friends and family, but cannot handle cooking for a large crowd, consider holding a potluck instead. That way, everyone can bring their favorite comfort foods and share them, which makes everything even more hyggelig.

When it comes to drinks, any hot drinks like coffee, tea, or hot chocolate can add to a hyggelig atmosphere. The essential drink in Denmark is glogg, or spiced mulled wine for hygge. Again, find what works for you. There is nothing cozier than sitting indoors with a steaming cup in your hand, and it is a simple pleasure that costs pennies.

Potluck Ideas

Sometimes, you do not have enough time to cook or that you just don't know what to cook. No matter how hard we plan ahead, there will always be one of those moments when we feel lost. What do you do, especially if you are cooking for a crowd of people gathering for a cozy evening? No, not Chinese food takeout. Consider the old neighborhood dinner swaps.

The best thing about a dinner swap is that you do not need to worry about cooking dinner. If you have a trustworthy neighbor, they can do you a favor and cook a little extra just for you so you can have the evening to relax. When it is time for you to return the favor, just choose delicious, simple recipes that are easy to double. It takes little effort to turn a one-family dinner into a two-family dinner.

Moreover, dinner swaps will save you a lot of money on your grocery bill. If you plan out five different meals ahead, you will forget to add certain ingredients when you cook, and then they go to waste. Moreover, you need to go to the store often, which is not healthy for your fuel economy, and you also need to spend more on fresh ingredients.

Alexandra Jessen

When you rotate meals in a dinner swap, you can buy bulk foods, cook everything, and you're done! Simple! With that said, there are several ways you can structure your dinner swap.

As mentioned earlier, the first way is to collaborate with a neighbor. Set up an agreement in which you agree to cook a hot meal for them once or twice a week if they do the same to you. Reciprocity is a part of hygge, after all. Not only that you do not need to worry about cooking on that day, but you also foster a good relationship with your neighbor.

Alternatively, you can also have multiple neighbors joining the party. You can spend an afternoon cooking for four or even five families and drop the food off at their place and pick one up for yourself. Make sure that everyone cooks dishes that can be frozen easily so you can put them in the freezer until you need to eat them. This is a great idea because you only need to spend an afternoon cooking, and then you are set for the rest of the week. That sounds like a bargain!

Of course, you do not need to restrict your cooking party to your neighbors. If you have a weekly or monthly book club, propose this idea to them. If your children areon a sports team, why not talk to other parents on the team? Arrange to have dinners swapped before or after the game. You can also arrange potluck with your friends, colleagues, and family members. It's also worth pointing out that the dinner you cook does not need to be costly.

Hygge

Simplicity is an important part of hygge, after all. Cooking in bulk is a great solution.

If you are serious about all of this, and you have a group of people who want to be involved, set up a meeting first, ideally in person but planning things outin Skype's video chat is okay if everyone is busy. The point of the meeting is to get to know each other, set expectations and schedules well in advance to prevent any troubles.

When planning, determine who will cook which days, when will the meals be swapped, family sizes, will dinner include desserts, price range, the container for the food, and confirm if anyone is a vegetarian or if anyone has any allergies.

Then, you need to plan out a menu because everyone can remain organized, not to mention that everyone will cook a different meal. Before showing up for the meeting, ask everyone to think of several meals they would like to cook for the potluck. From there, have one person write out who will cook what, on which day, every week on the calendar. Try to plan out at least a month in advance.

Other than that, keep an eye out for special discounts or grocery store food coupons to save some extra money. Plan your dinner based on what is on sale. You can also plan your meal around the ingredients that are in season. Purchase produce at farmer's markets or community supported agriculture farms are also a good way to keep the cost down. Finally, make sure that everyone in your group like similar food. If you like vegetarian or organic meals, then start a group with similar tastes and preferences.

Books

Reading detaches yourself from the busy, fast-paced modern world, making reading hygge. You can bump up the hygge factor by curling up on a couch with your book and blanket. In warm weather, sitting outside under the tree reading is hygge as well.

Games

Another hygge way to spice up your evening is hosting a game night. Tabletop games are a good way to have fun with your friends and family at home. There is no involvement nor distractions from technology. This gives you three things about hygge: companionship, relaxation, and simplicity.

Another fun activity you should consider is a sing-along. It may sound like something straight from the 60s, but it is still a common activity in Denmark. Many Danish households have many copies of folk songbooks. They sing those songs to affirm the ideas of simplicity, community, belonging, cheerfulness, and reciprocity. There is an American equivalent of these books called

"Rise Up Singing" that contains lyrics and chords for all kinds of singable songs.

Snuggle

Of course, there are only a few things cozier than cuddling. It combines all the good things about hygge like comfort, simplicity, and companionship. It is free, warm, and joyful. You can do it with your friends, pets, or your loved ones.

Scents

In addition to food bringing hygge into your life, you can also incorporate it using scents as well because taste and smell always go hand-in-hand. Since we have talked extensively about food already, we might as well discuss how you can use scents to cozy up your living space. Just like tastes, scents are also a powerful memory trigger, so the smell of apple pie might remind you when your mum used to bake one even before you eat it. When you do, you are reminded of that fond, tender time again.

While there is no sure-fire way that one smell will bring hygge into your life, you can use your past experience as clues to help you figure out which scent you should use. People have different past experience and so the scent that they associate their memory with also differ from person to person. Still, you should look for all of the smells that remind you of safety and being cared for. It should allow you to let loose and relax. Certain smells such as the smell of cooking, the smell of a certain place we perceive as safe, or the smell of a blanket you use at home can be very hyggelig because they remind us when we felt completely safe. So, when selecting a scent, think which one makes you feel safe and cared for or which one brings you back to your childhood innocence? Again, these fragrances are different from person to person, so take some time to identify which scents connect to you. Here are some ideas:

Campfires might remind you of the Fourth of July. The smell of charcoal grill might remind you of dinner in the summertime. You might associate chlorine swimming pool to summertime. Fallen leaves might remind you of making leaf piles and leaf houses. The smell of freshly baked caramel rolls might remind you of your grandma's house, your cousin, or the fun time. Maybe your father used to cook you some soup. Library books might remind you of your childhood. Lilacs could bring about the memory of spring. New crayons might make you think of your time in school or kindergarten, signaling a new beginning, innocence, and creativity. The smell of pine might remind you of Christmas time. Popcorn might make you think of the time when you and your family binge-watch movies together. Rosemary and thyme could remind you of the garden you used to tend to as a kid. The smell of sunscreen might make you think of the beach or the best spring and summer vacation you ever have. Warm hay might make you think of the time you went horseback riding or camping.

Other hygge scents include the ocean, chocolate, flowers, rain, new car, cinnamon, freshly washed clothes, lavender, Thanksgiving dinner, hot cookies fresh from the oven, bacon, coffee, vanilla, and freshly baked bread.

So, if scents can bring you warm hygge feelings, how can you incorporate them into your lives regularly? How can we maintain hygge without keeping a Christmas tree in your home all year long? There are a few different approaches.

The Real Deal

Thankfully, you can experience some of these comforting hygge scents first hand. For example, you can enjoy the smell of coffee or freshly baked bread or cookie by making them. Buy fresh flowers, fry some bacon, or pop some popcorn and then savor the aroma. Therefore, you can surround yourself with these natural hygge scents regularly so you can evoke the feelings of comfort, familiarity,and coziness easily.

Essential Oils and Diffusers

When you cannot experience the scents firsthand easily, using diffusers might be your best bet. You should invest in cold air diffusers and essential oils. So, when you want comfort from the smell of pumpkin spice, natural pine, lavender, or warm vanilla, you can just create the perfect hygge atmosphere.

Lotions or Perfumes

Perhaps you find comfort in your mother's perfume because she used to be by your side all the time, making you feel safe and loved. Perhaps you have a nostalgic memory of a particular Bath and Body Works fragrance. You can use lotions and perfumes in addition to essential oils to create hygge easily.

Hygge on a Budget

Sometimes, you might be on a tight budget but still want to enjoy the hygge experience. While there are many useful ideas in this book, you should only practice those that are most convenient for you. You certainly do not need to go out of your way to attain coziness. Here are some simple ideas:

Candle Routine

When you search "hygge" online, candles will always be there. This is normal since the Danes are obsessed with candles. However, if you want to burn as many candles as the Danes, it can get expensive. So, what do you do? Well, you can cut down and not burn every single candle in your home at once. Try to have three candles ready at any time and go through a cycle of lighting one at a time throughout the day when you are at home. You can buy candles in bulk on the clearance shelves for relatively cheap prices.

Slow Cooking

It is a worthy investment. Think of hearty soups, chilies, beans, curries, stews, etc. Everything just tastes a lot better when it has been stewing and developing its delectable flavors for hours. You can make large batches of cheap but healthy food that can last at least a few days. Winter is the perfect time to experiment with new slow cooker recipes.

Books

Why buy when you can borrow? You can visit your local library to get a few books for your reading sessions. Combine that with a blanket, a mug of something hot, lit candles or a fireplace or soft lighting and hardly anything is more hyggelig than this. You can use reading to combat screen addiction too.

Non-Caffeinated Hot Beverages

While the idea of hot cacao might be a good one, you can never go wrong with other, non-caffeinated options as well. Besides, drinking caffeinated drinks might make it harder for you to relax. So, instead of investing a few bucks on coffee, get yourself a variety of warming beverages to suit whatever mood you have.

Chill

Sometimes, all that you need to attain a state of hygge is just slowing down. Some people are just high-strung and perpetually hectic. Relaxing might be difficult for you because you feel that you need to be productive all the time and you feel guilty when you are not. So, what do you do then?

Start by giving yourself permission to procrastinate. Yes, you should not procrastinate, but come on. You have been working your head off for a long time. Surely, you deserve a break. While that to-do list will not clear itself, you can be sure that it will not go anywhere either. Sit down and write down what is on your mind so you can free it up momentarily. You will get to those tasks later. Just appreciate the atmosphere without needing to fill the time or avoid boredom. Then, perhaps take the time to pick up a book and read a few pages. Try out the new recipe you found or just enjoy that hot drink you fixed for yourself. Maybe watch something while you're at it. It is okay to take a break sometimes because it is good for your mental wellbeing. The things you want to get done can wait a bit longer. They are not going anywhere. Besides, sometimes the best thing to do is nothing at all.

Hygge at Work

While incorporating hygge at home involves simple decorations, lighting, scents, candles, and other basic things, bringing hygge to work is a different story. Still, you definitely should bring it to work to completely live a hygge lifestyle. Before you try out any of these, consult with your supervisor to make sure that you do not violate any internal rules and regulations, or tick off your coworkers (especially the one sitting closest to you). Here are a few ideas:

Starting your day with a warm drink is as hygge as it gets, followed up by a cool drink in the afternoon. So, invest in a good hot and cold thermos. Freeze a nutrient dense smoothie overnight and let it thaw in the morning. Bring along home-baked breakfast cookies to work. Why? Well, to share with your colleagues, of course! Hygge is also about lifting up other's spirits as well.

When you have cool and warm beverage right at home, you can save some money to buy a stainless steel lunchbox instead of loading up your coffee card. You can put last night's dinner or your favorite cozy comfort food in the lunchbox. That way, meals will be exciting and you can eat healthier more often. Having a freeze-able lunch bag is also a good idea as well because you can keep fruits and drinks cool, not to mention that you can bring perishable meals and snacks with you.

When the work stress gets to you, you might just need to take a short break. If possible, go outside for five minutes or so and sit down somewhere. Then, focus on no checking our phone and just breathe. Let your eyes rest. IF you work in an office, or in a high-rise building, then standing by the window is good enough. Gaze outside often to let your eyes rest and stand up as often as possible. How is this hygge? Well, you pamper yourself and taking care of yourself by being aware of the signals in your body, not to mention that all of these things are healthy.

The Desk

In addition, you could also try to make your workplace itself more pleasant so you can enjoy working more. If possible, you should also consider bringing a vase to your office and keep a fresh flower in it. You can also invest a lamp with an incandescent bulb to counter the blue light coming from the fluorescent light and the light from the monitor. To remain comfortable, consider bringing a cushy scarf or jacket with you to work. Put them on the back of your chair to combat the cool office temperature or stiff chairs. You can also put it on your lap, turning them into a makeshift blanket. You can also try switching your shoes and wear something comfortable like your favorite sneakers. If it doesn't violate the internal rules, not a lot of people will question you about it anyway. Also, to help you focus and relaxed, you can try listening to something. You can put together a list of calming songs or music, or listen to white noise or any ambience that you like the best. All it takes is a quick search on YouTube.

Cozying Up

While we are on the topic of making the eight hours' period of working pleasant, you can also bring a scented salve for your tired hands. Have a cup of plain, warm water with you while you work. Take a sip from it occasionally and let the warmth and plainness of it all to soothe you. If you want something sweet, bring an apple or any fruit that you enjoy eating to work with you. A cup of coffee in the afternoon is never better than fruits anyway.

Since hygge is all about getting comfortable, if possible, try to wear really comfortable clothing. Some companies might not be too strict about the dress code, but chances are that you need to look good while being uncomfortable at the same time. Still, even if you go into the office in heels, do your very best to be comfortable at the desk. Many people spend eight hours a day there, so might as well make the most out of it.

If your office is open and spacious, consider making the space feels more intimate. Put a comfy chair close to the bookcase or try working in a small room or office from time to time. Also, try switching up meeting locations. If you do not need to meet up at the conference room, try going to a care or host the meeting in the common area. Try finding smaller area and sit closer to your colleagues.

Talk More

Personal connection is an important element of hygge, plus it makes everyone feels welcomed at the workplace. This is what a good job is about. It is not about the pay, but about the people, the connection. This can be difficult for introverts, even if they want to talk to other people.

Still, try to schedule brief weekly check-ins with your favorite colleagues to ensure that the connection is still there, even if you are busy. These people are your go-to gut check, or cheerleader. While you are at it, you should also stay connected with your coworkers who are working remotely. They might need help creating and maintaining personal connections, so do them a favor and reach out.

If you want to get to know other colleagues better, consider inviting them to a 30-minute one-on-one talk. You can invite them to a quick coffee, a lunchroom catch-up, or a simple Skype chat. You don't really need an agenda here, but do think of a few things you want to talk about to keep the conversation going.

Potluck

Because comfort food is the source of all things hygge, what is a better way to savor home-cooked food than with your best colleagues by your side and having a taste of each other's food? The idea is eating together with your colleagues to encourage the feeling of belonging and closeness. Better yet, organize a potluck day rather than bringing lunch yourself. When everyone shares, everyone gets hygge.

Random Acts of Kindness

You can make someone's day just by being kind to your co-workers. It does not need to be anything big. Bringing a box of donuts to the office or giving them a compliment for a job well done is enough. Working can become stressful very quickly, and social support help everyone copes with that. After all, being vulnerable with someone opens up the possibility for a huge distribution of the stress we all experience.

Teamwork

In the workplace, teamwork is crucial. Team spirit is also a part of the Danish culture because they used to work in groups since childhood. They are taught to give help or seek one when they need it, and they are also encouraged to remain confident despite their weaknesses. They are also taught to be humble despite their strengths as well.

The spirit of cooperation and teamwork is often seen in all aspects of the Danish life, in the classroom, workplace, and at home. When you have a family that you can depend on like a team, you feel a deep sense of belonging. The same can be said in the workplace as well. So, it is worth trying to organize team-building activities to encourage teamwork, such as scavenger hunts to tournaments.

Finally, be in the present and allow yourself the time to take care of yourself throughout the day. Visiting the restroom to wash your face so you could freshen up. Do it once an hour if you want. Again, if your job requires you to sit around for eight hours a day, you will need to stand up as often as possible. Also, have lunch elsewhere other than your desk some days just to keep things interesting. Eat out with your colleagues and connect with them.

Hygge While Traveling

While hygge seems to paint a picture of you staying inside your candle-lit home reading a book by the fireplace, hygge itself is not limited to your home. In fact, it has no physical limits. It can be practiced everywhere, even while you are traveling. While you might see traveling is the opposite of hygge, there are actually plenty of ways you can practice it on-the-go. So, here are how you can have a hygge holiday.

Destination

First, you need to know where you want to go. We will talk about this more extensively in a later chapter. The basic idea is that you need to know how much time you have, who you want to bring with you, how much money you have, what kind of vacation you want, and what you want to do. Only then can you start choosing your destination.

Hotel

Next, you should stay in a hygge-inspired hotel. Sometimes, though, you might not need a hotel. You can also rent a cabin, cottage, or use Airbnb to find a place to stay. If you decide to go for Airbnb, though, you should be careful because there could be problems involved. At the same time, you will not find a hygge-inspired place to stay most of the time, so try to make the most out of what you have.

Food

This is a pretty straightforward thing as well. While most Nordic cuisine is hygge such as Danish pastries, fihs, porridge, meatballs, or veggie-heavy plates, you can always eat the food that you just enjoy. While you're at it, make sure to drink warm drinks as well. Most of the time, your destination will always have a coffee shop, so take some time and just chill there with a cup of coffee. Alternatively, go to the local pub and have a drink. The idea is to distance yourself from the chaos of the world and just enjoy the present moment.

Clothing

There are not a lot of things you need to do here. Just wear anything that is comfortable and minimalist. In fact, this is perfect for traveling because you will always be packing light. Speaking of packing, make sure to bring some scented candles for your travel. It does not have to be much, but try to burn at least one candle a day.

30-Day Challenge

Okay, so you know all the fun activities and things you can bring into your home to make it more hyggelig. As with anything, starting is the challenge. By now, you might know what you can do to being hygge into your life, but you might not know how to start. We have you covered. This section will help you transition from your normal lifestyle to a hygge lifestyle in thirty days. These are just ideas to help you ease into the hygge life. You can only do one of them for each day. That is fine. But if you are a completionist, then do all of them if you want.

For day 1, we can start with something simple. You can either start writing a gratitude journal, detailing everything that you are, well, grateful for, or you can make your favorite coffee or hot drink and enjoy it while sitting outside. Hey, if you want, you can enjoy a hot drink outside while you are writing a gratitude journal.

For day 2, you can start enjoying a hot drink in a local, cozy café. Alternatively, you can hang up fairy lights somewhere in your home to get a cozy feeling. Again, you can combine the two because any cozy café has cozy lighting, although they do not go as far as lighting candles.

On day 3, you can invite a friend or a family member over to enjoy your favorite movie, or spend an hour to declutter your own home. That, or you can contact an old friend by phone or Facebook. Spend some time to catch up with them, and if possible, invite them over for a movie night.

On day 4, have breakfast at your favorite coffee place. Consider revisiting that coffee place on day 2. If you don't want to, you can start your morning with stretches and a cup of coffee. At the end of the day, try to spend an evening watching a movie and relax alone.

Hygge

For day 5, enjoy your own company for a day, or for an hour. While you're at it, try to make a homemade gift for a loved one. That or put up lanterns in your home for cozy lighting.

For day 6, you can enjoy another's company again by inviting a friend over for coffee. Give them a hug or give your pillow a loving hug because, for some people, your pillow is always there to wipe your tears. If you do not want to have someone over, you can do something you loved as a child like spending some time in the backyard looking through the nooks and cranny and clean up the place. Alternatively, you can relive your childhood memory by doing the things you love as a child. Maybe you can break out that Lego toys you have but never have the time to assemble.

On day 7, go for a walk and enjoy nature. Along the way, stop by a cozy café to get your hot drink fix. Then, why not try to spend some time making a list of things that make you happy?

For day 8, organize a game night with your family and friends. Again, if you feel tired at the end of the day and just want time to yourself, you can pick up a book and read as much as you can.

For day 9, you can decorate your own home and relax by the fire or candlelight.

On day 10, why not try baking your favorite cake? While you are at it, put on your favorite soothing music.

Alexandra Jessen

On day 11, spend the day not touching anything with an internet connection and spend the time pampering yourself.

For day 12, plan a dinner with your friends and have them come over and help you fix dinner. You can also have fun with them by letting them help you in making a hygge corner in your home so everyone can just chill there.

For day 13, bake cookies just because you can. Save those cookies at the end of the 30-day period as a prize, or enjoy them while you read your favorite book, wrapped up in your favorite blanket.

On day 14, try meditating for fifteen minutes straight. If you are used to meditating for five or ten minutes, then this is a good way to bump the number up. If you already doing fifteen minutes' sessions daily, then you can try to go for twenty minutes. If you are too restless, spend some time coloring.

On day 15, spend an evening watching movie and just chill. Turn off your phone or put it on silence mode, and leave it in another room and fully enjoy the movie. You can also go down the Memory Lane by looking at old photos.

For day 16, try wearing slippers all day (no socks!), or try your cooking skill and bake some bread. You can also take the time to write a letter to someone you miss. Too old-fashioned? Then just send them a message through Facebook or whatever platform you two are connected and spend the evening catching up.

For day 17, take yourself outside for a walk in the park or wood to enjoy nature's gift. Then, on the way back, buy yourself some flowers to add more colors in your home. If it is cold outside, spend the evening by the fire.

On day 18, book nothing in for the day. Spend the day however you want. Enjoy and live the day, not caring about tomorrow.

On day 19, you can try baking something new, or watch the sunrise while cuddling a loved one. They can be a pet, a person, or a pillow. Whatever works.

For day 20, pamper yourself by taking a bubble bath. Spend about an hour or so in it, without any digital distractions. If you want, try cooking yourself a main meal from scratch to complete the evening.

For day 21, you can try introducing a new but familiar smell into your home with essential oils. You can also scent up the whole house by cooking your favorite comfort food.

On day 22, invite your friends over to chat, play video games, or watch movies together using candlelights to set the mood.

On day 23, if it is warm outside, spend the time outside and sit in the sun, soaking in the sunlight. Alternatively, do yoga by the candlelight. You can also take the time to declutter your email by deleting irrelevant emails.

For day 24, go for a walk in nature in the woods or by the lake. Sit down at a bench somewhere and listen to your favorite songs while you enjoy nature.

For day 25, try going out for a picnic, take a yoga class or Tai Chi class to unwind.

On day 26, take the time to declutter your home, or make a gift for a loved one.

On day 27, pick or buy some flowers and put them in vases, or watch your favorite show.

For day 28, listen to some soothing music. Alternatively, look at the gratitude journal and practice being grateful for the things listed in the book.

For day 29, bake some cookies and share them with your neighbors or your loved one. If you do the latter, make sure to cuddle them at the end of the day.

Finally, on day 30, take a nap, clear your schedule, relax and congratulate yourself, and repeat.

Hygge and Relationships

The Danes know something to keep them happy. They also know how to maintain a happy marriage. These facts are cemented by the fact that they are among the happiest countries in the world. Hygge is about consciously creating a pleasant life and it extends to marriage by creating content and satisfying partnerships. There are a few reasons why the Danes are happier than the American in their marriages based on hygge.

Cozy Home

Hygge creates a cozy home, and the Danes value a cozy home. The country is enveloped in the cold and darkness most time of the year. The Danes are great at creating a cozy and happy home. Because they spend a lot of time indoors, after all. So, creating a cozy home is very personal to them. Relaxingliving space is crucial to them. Many of them are creating this invisible cozy spirit that characterizes hygge in their homes because they need a safe haven to relax and cheer up. If you come back to a cozy home, you will feel that lovely and positive energy that takes away your stress, making you happy and forget about that 8-hour work. That means you are in a more agreeable mood after coming from work, which minimizes conflict between you and your spouse.

Alexandra Jessen

Drama

For some reason, many people flock to drama just about anything. The Danes are not immune to the toxic temptation of drama, but they certainly know how to minimize its effect. They do their best to not whine and complain while focusing on the positive in conversations with their loved one. That, however, does not mean that they never fight. They fight, but they do so to solve a problem. They never fight to win, but they do so to keep dramas out of their lives. If you want to enjoy hygge with your partner, you should put your everyday drama at the door. It is difficult, but it gets easier as time passes. By then, it is a lot easier to be kinder to your loved one.

Weddings

Weddings in Denmark are often low-key affairs that take place at the town hall without any elaborate ceremonies. They marry then they are in their thirties, and they know that they have invested enough in their own lives to be sure that they are financially secured going into a marriage. After all, poverty is the cause of many divorces, and children should not have to suffer through poverty. What part of this is hygge? It is the fact that they take things slow by not marrying in their twenties without a stable income.

Together-Time

You might often see couples sitting at the dinner table, not talking to one another, and have their noses stuck to their phones. This is a sad reality that we live in, and the Danes are well aware of that. When they decide to spend time together, they mean it. That involves putting away their phones and going to the park, walking side by side, hand in hand. They make sure that they concentrate on their significant other.

While they are at it, they enjoy the small things together. It is about taking pleasure in the soothing, gentle, yet seemingly insignificant things in life. It is hygge to have dinners with your friends or your family. It is just a part of Danish life. Hygge is about being kind to yourself and those around you, after all. This basically makes you a better partner.

Tradition

Danish families have a shared culture, unique to the household. A couple grows stronger together if they have a system to implement certain traditions together where hygge is included. Shared values translate into powerful routines that can be maintained easily. This allows the existence of a unique culture that works to positively influence the entire household.

Alexandra Jessen

Divorce

While Danish couples are happier than most in the world, they are not immune to divorce. In fact, Denmark has the fourth highest divorce rate in Europe, but they go out quietly. Divorces are cheap and painless. It is so convenient that you can file for divorce online. But why is it that when Danish couples divorce, they go out quietly? You can thank the high female employment and the strong social safety net for that. Plus, we mentioned earlier that Danes do not get into marriage until they are secured economically, so a Danish divorce is not likely to become a nasty battle over money. If it is, then the entire process will be all the more painful and both sides will hold a grudge against each other. Moreover, divorces are not as acrimonious so stigma is not such a big problem. You can consider this to be a silver lining because most Danes who get divorced become friends with their ex-wife or ex-husband, and they get married again pretty soon. So, you can say that there are no hard feelings between the husband and the wife. In fact, some of then go as far as celebrate their divorce anniversary together with beers and a lovely meal with their new partners!

Creating a Healthy Relationship with Hygge

Now that you know how the Danes are happy in their marriage (or even after one), let us look at how you can build a healthy relationship with hygge.

Communication

One can never stress enough the importance of clear communication, of open dialogue where both sides openly tell the other about how they truly feel. It promotes growth, understanding and ultimately leads to a healthy relationship. Open communication and the Danish lifestyle of comfort and familiarity go hand-in-hand. This is partly because of the fact that they leave the drama at the door. Hygge is about slowing down, taking your time, and freeing yourself from distractions. It is about focusing all of your senses to the present, to your immediate surroundings and stay that way. This is the perfect environment for a serious conversation. Moreover, hygge and healthy conversation establishes a positive feedback loop. Hygge creates the feeling of harmony, belonging, and shared experience, which paves way for open communication. When you engage in open dialogue, you feel comfortable in engaging deeper conversation, which results in a stronger feeling of hygge and connection. So, how do you create a hygge conversation? Simple.

First, turn off all distractions like mobile phones or television. Engage and focus fully on the dialogue. Remember to take things slow. Do not rush the discussion. Make decisions only when you feel that you are ready. Most of the time, that happens after the dialogue so do not make decisions when you do not have all the details. While talking, get comfortable, both physically and mentally because hygge is all about comfort. Open up, share your ideas and be respectful of others because a conversation is a two-way street. Of course, light candles because that is hygge.

While we are on the topic of communication, it is worth diving deeper into the subject because it is more to communication than that. In fact, many relationships fail because of the lack of communication which often leads to misunderstandings. This can cause many bad things to happen such ad resentment for each other, cheating, drug or alcohol abuse, and many more. To avoid all of these problems, here are the ten ways to improve your communication.

Time and Place

You might be familiar with the phrase, "This is neither the time nor the place," Keeping this simple statement in mind helps you a lot when you want to have an important conversation. After all, you want to make sure that your partner is receptive whenever you bring up a serious topic. Make sure you make the conversation happen in an environment without any distraction and you two have enough time to discuss the problem.

Hygge

For instance, bringing up the budgeting problem while your partner is getting the kids ready for school probably is not a good idea because you might have only fifteen minutes to talk about it. Instead, tell your partner in advance that you wish to discuss the problem after the children go to sleep tonight. That way, your partner has the time to think about the problem and both of you can set aside a specific time to talk about the issue.

Remove Distractions

Now that you have set up a time and place to talk with your partner, it is time to free yourself from distractions. Unfortunately, it is a lot easier said than done. We live in a society that runs on distractions. Our phones chip with every notification from Facebook, text, tweet, and posts from Instagram. Our watches also ping when we got a new mail or vibrate if we have been sitting for a while (if you can afford one, that is). Our email inboxes will be chock-full of work emails, calendar, memos, and many more, not to mention the ads you need to unsubscribe from.

So, when you finally sit down with your partner to talk about the problem, banish those distractions. Switch off the TV, and your computer. Put your phone in another room. Everyone knows what it feels like talking to another person who only listens to you partially while they respond to texts, checking their newsfeed, and doing other things on their phone. It hurts to be second in their priority list. In fact, some listenershave to put in the effort to partially listen. Many might just outright nod and "mhmhm" their way to the end of the conversation without hearing a word from you. This is not genuine listening. So, if you want effective communication, make sure to leave distractions at the door and fully engage in the conversation.

Just remember that communication is a two-way street. A conversation involves both speaking and listening. Here are some ways to ensure that you are successful in both.

Take Your Time

Sometimes, when someone is discussing something that is interesting to them or that when they have an idea that they cannot wait to share, their speech increases exponentially. While this encourages them to speak, they do not know how to string their ideas properly. They will most likely race through their ideas without thinking about what they want to say or how they want to say it specifically. We all have been there.

When that happens, the best thing that could happen is confusion. So, you need to spend more time explaining your ideas. The worst thing that could happen is when both sides of the conversation are arguing and the conversation gets heated. Tempers will flare, ideas get muddled and feelings will take over. Eventually, one side will say something that they will later regret. Of course, both of these situations are not ideal.

So, when you have a conversation with your significant other, take your time. Hygge is, after all, about conscious engagement with the present, so you should take your time. Do not rush through everything. Think carefully about what you want to say, and remember that it is never a bad idea to pause and structure your response properly. Taking a bit of time now would save both sides from the pain of more explanation or arguments later.

"I" vs. "You"

This is a very effective strategy when you are discussing an issue that you want to resolve. If you are talking to your friend or loved ones about their habit of canceling at the last minute, for example, never say "Why do you always cancel on me?" While many people would structure their questions this way, you might spot the two trigger words that might spark an argument.

The problem is the use of two words "you" and "always," When you use the word "you", you are accusing the other person while the word "always" put unnecessary stress, making the accusation feels more like a personal attack. That will not be well-received by the recipient. So, what can be done differently?

Instead, try flipping the script around. Do not point out their faulty behavior and focus on how her behavior, regardless of right or wrong it is, makes you feel. Why is their behavior a problem for you? In our example, you could instead say "I feel let down when our plans get canceled last minute. I'm just so excited to spend time with you, you know? What can we do to make it work?" You see? Suddenly, the tone of the question is softened significantly. Moreover, you are only voicing out how you feel so the other person cannot feel attacked. In doing so, you put yourself on the other person's side and you make it clear that you just want to solve this problem with them.

Stay Focused

Whatever topics you are discussing, remain focused on the main idea. It is actually very easy to trail off to subtopics that are not relevant to the main idea. While discussing the problem and its details is good, but just make sure that both of you are on the same page about the most important things first.

Non-verbal Cues

There are many studies out there that highlight the importance of body language in communication. Some have argued that more than 90% of our communication is done non-verbally such as nodding. Regardless of the numbers, it is worth remembering that words can only deliver so much information. A majority of the information lies in the non-verbal cues – the body language, tone, pitch, etc. After all, you can interpret a question differently based on the tone. Here is an example, "Where is my key?" sounds innocent enough, but when you yell "Where's my key!?" at another person, it implies that you are angry and that you suspect that the person you are yelling at has stolen your key. See the difference?

So, pay attention to the body language of the other person. Look at their face and observe their reaction. Look at how they place their arms. Observe how they lean their body. All of these are clues that tell you more about how they react to your ideas so you know how to proceed.

At the same time, you need to also be aware of your own body language. So, when you are talking to your significant other, look at them in the eyes to show them that you are listening. Do not cross your arms. Put them somewhere you are comfortable to let them know that you are open to their ideas. Lean forward and try to show interest in what they have to say. Nod to show that you are following and understanding what they are saying. All of these things are minuscule, but they help a lot in a productive discussion.

Of course, you should also watch for you and their tone of voice as well. Think of a simple "sure" can suggest. If you say "sure" clearly in an upbeat voice, you are showing the other person that you wholly and enthusiastically agree with them. A long, drawn-out "suuuuure" suggests that you are being sarcastic, or suspicious of them. An infamous response "I'm fine," also falls into this category because many people say that they are fine when they really are not fine. So, when you are talking with your partner, watch your tone of voice because it gives context to your response and it adds so much more meaning to your response.

Being Open-minded

It is critical to have an open and flexible mindset if you want to have a productive conversation, whether you are speaking or listening. While both of you might not agree on an idea or issue, having an open mind ensures that you understand and able to empathize with the other person's perspective. Moreover, if you initiate the conversation with an open mind, it is a lot easier to reach a compromise.

Patience

It is one of the greatest virtues a human can have. We all know that many conversations can be frustrating and it is difficult to maintain your patience during those moments. However, patience is critical for success. How can you remain patient having a frustrating conversation? One way to do so is reminding yourself that you both are on the same side, trying to solve a problem. The fact that you both have strong opinions about the problem shows that you two genuinely care about and that you two share some common ground. So, focus on that commonality. Both of you may need to compromise a bit but always keep the most important thing in mind. You will eventually find a solution.

At the same time, you might need to take a break from the conversation to maintain that patience. That is totally alright because when things get heated, you should take a short break to allow things to simmer down. There is no point trying to rush to the solution and risk sparking arguments that harm the relationship. If you do decide to take a break, discuss with your partner about the date, time, and place you two can return to the topic. Not only that this allows both sides to cool down, but it also gives you two enough time to think. Thinking is just as important in a conversation as speaking. Use the time wisely to try and understand your partner's perspective. That way, you can continue to communicate effectively the next time you reconvene. Using all of the tips above, you should be able to reach your end-goal of understanding, acceptance, and compromise without harming the relationship.

Connection

While connection or companionship is an important part of hygge, technology is definitely not hygge. While technology has connected people all over the world, it has separated people physically.

Hygge is all about spending quality time with people. It involves real conversation and enjoying each other's company. Basically, we have a basic need to feel connected with others. This is simply a part of our biology because we are social creatures. We have the need to feel close to someone and we need to feel loved and cared about. These things keep us going in the difficult times. Basically, we are happy if we have a good, healthy relationship. So, how can hygge create those connections?

Hygge is choosing rustic over new things. It is enjoying the simple things in life rather than the posh things with all the bells and whistles. It is about savoring the ambiance rather than the excitement. Hygge is all about being humble. It is about unhurried calm. So, if you want to find ways to create a connection with your loved ones through hygge, keep these values in mind.

But what do you do if the connection you are trying to make is not well-received or shot down by the other person? For example, what if you plan a Fredagshygge night (a hygge family night) but one of your children or your significant other does not feel like it? What if you try to make that connection, but the other person is pulling away?

Because many things you do can be considered to be hygge, start by thinking about their interests. Using the conversation tips we discussed previously, find out what they want to do as a family. While they might be interested in board games tonight, they might be interested in having a campfire or a movie night.

Engaging in an activity together is also effective because the conversation can flow naturally in these circumstances. For example, plan and make dinner together or work on a project or craft. If the approaches we discussed are not effective, then there might be an underlying issue with the current relationship that has nothing to do with hygge. Again, you might need to have a serious conversation with your significant other. If that fails too, you might need some help, ideally from a professional, to help rebuild the relationship.

Cooperation

Another important aspect of hygge living is cooperation (in addition to the other 5 c's: comfort, connection, coziness, conversation, and candles) is cooperation. Hygge is all about helping out, doing your part and helping out.

In an essence, hygge is togetherness which we all want no matter how young or old we are. If you have friends over for dinner, it is actually alright to ask them for a helping hand in the kitchen. In fact, it is great if you do that because you can be connected with your friends while everyone is making dinner. Besides, it feels lonely to leave your friends waiting for you in the dining room while you fix them dinner. If you feel like it, take it a step further and make it a potluck so everyone shares in the experience. It is actually more hyggelig if everyone helps out in the kitchen to prepare food instead of having the host in the kitchen alone.

At the same time, if you are telling stories or engaged in a conversation, try to listen more than you speak. At least, try to speak as much as you listen. Shared experience, cooperation, and equality all fall under the hygge umbrella. So, make sure everyone feels that their voice is being heard by giving them room to speak up.

So, as we move toward establishing solid, healthy relationships, allocating times for loved ones, and practicing work-life balance, make sure to keep the hygge philosophy in mind. Make sure to remain engaged in the conversation and participate in activities that build or strengthen the connection. Cooperate to foster togetherness.

Date Night Ideas

Because hygge does not involve extravagant dinner, there are plenty of fun activities you can do right at home. Here are some ideas:

Play "Would You Rather?"

The game is engaging yet simple. It can be a great way to have a laugh after a stressful day. Sometimes, it can also spark important conversations. While the game in itself is not as exciting, you can use it in combination with other games from this section to have a fun night ahead of you. Moreover, you can use it to start a conversation as well because you can always follow the question up by asking why. You might get some interesting answers and learn more about the person you are talking to.Here are twenty questions to start with:

Would you rather be in prison for four years for something you did not do, or get away with something terrible that you did but always live in fear of being caught?

Would you rather be able to see ten minutes into your own future, or ten minute into the future of anyone but not yourself?

Would you rather be ten minutes late all the time, or be twenty minutes early all the time?

Would you rather never use social media ever again, or never watch another movie or TV show?

Hygge

Would you rather live in the real world, or in a virtual one where all your wishes come true?

Would you rather live without heating or AC, or without the internet?

Would you rather be poor but help people, or become insanely rich by hurting people?

Would you rather be loved by all, or feared by all?

Would you rather travel 500 years into the future, or the past?

Would you rather have an unlimited supply of taco for life, or sushi for life?

Would you rather eat rice every meal, or bread every meal?

Would you rather spend ten years in China, or Russia?

Would you rather never feel cold again, or never sweat again?

Would you rather be covered in scales, or in fur?

Would you rather live in a tree house, or in a cave?

Would you rather never have to do the dishes, or clean the bathroom again?

Would you rather have free Wi-Fi wherever you go, or never run out of battery power?

Would you rather be able to make more than $3,500 a month, or be in debt for $100,000?

Would you rather believe a comforting lie, or know the uncomfortable truth?

Would you rather humans go to Mars, or the moon?

There are literally hundreds of thousands of questions out there. In fact, there is an app to help you generate these silly yet fun questions. Just remember that if you do use an electronic device in this game, make sure to use it sparingly.

Plan Your Next Vacation

While planning does not sound so fun, taking the evening thinking of all the fun things you want to do for the next holiday can be a good way to relieve stress. Spending time brainstorming locations, activities, travel dates, etc. is not only fun, but you are saving yourself time because you can actually follow through with your plans. It is just fun to dream about it, after all, even if you do not actually follow through.

So, how do you plan your next vacation? There are six simple but critical questions you need to consider while you are planning your holiday. Now, you might think that the first question would be the location. Actually, the location is the least of your concern on the list. First, start by asking yourself how much time do you actually have. How long is the vacation going to last? A weekend? A week? A month? Determining how long your vacation will take decide what you can do and where you can go. If you only have four days off, then you should not spend half of it traveling the world.

The second question is about the kind of vacation you are looking for. What do you want from your vacation? Do you want a relaxing getaway or are you looking for an active adventure? What about a little of both? If you are the kind of person who cannot sit still for more than ten minutes, then going to the beach on some tropical island is not for you. You would be bored out of your mind within the first hour.

This leads us to the third question. So, ask yourself specifically what do you want to do on the vacation? Do you want to have a vigorous hike in the woods? Do you want to spend hours in the museum? Do you just want to sunbathe at the beach, drinking margaritas? You need to know what you are looking for because there are so many kinds of vacation.

Next, ask yourself who will be with you on the vacation. Will it be a solo adventure? Do you plan to bring your fiancé along? Will you be bringing all of your kids with you even though they are five years old? If your answer "yes" to the last question, you might not want to take long treks in the woods. So, make sure you know who will come along with you because they can make or break your vacation. Make sure everyone is on board with the vacation so everyone can have a good time.

Then, you need to know about your own budget. How much money are you willing to spend? This is a very important question. You can literally make it rain or you can be frugal in your budget planning. It all depends on where you go, what you want to do, whether you want to eat out each meal, or what time of the year you are taking your vacation. For example, if you want to go to Disney World during spring break, you will pay a premium compared to traveling in the peak of summer.

So, now that you know how much time you have, what type of vacation you want, what you want to do, who will be coming along, and how much you want to spend, you can proceed to select a destination. Where do you want to go? The previous five steps will help you decide because you know all the details already. Many people start with the location first and often stumble at the latter stages of the planning. After all, there are thousands of places you can visit, so how can you choose? Start small by answering the previous questions and you will be good to go.

Plan and Prepare Dinner

This might seem like an obvious option to some, but it can be very entertaining when everyone goes all-in and plan everything together. By everything, we mean everything. This involves peering over the cookbooks, grabbing the groceries and cooking the meal together. It is a very fun twist on the typical dinner at home. Of course, make sure to start this a little early in the afternoon if you do not want to eat at 10 pm. No one wants to get hangry (hungry and angry) on Fredagshygge night, and candles will not calm things down.

Top Chef

Another exciting twist on dinner at home is skipping the grocery shopping and planning altogether. You can take on the Master Chef-level of cookery challenge by selecting a specific ingredient that you have on hand, set a timer, and see what creative dish you can come up with. Just make sure to have some pizza coupons handy as Plan B in case things go awry.

Play Video Games

Again, practice moderation. Playing video games more than forty hours a week is bad, but playing it for one evening is alright. Actually, playing video games is super fun whether you are battling another in Wii tennis or spend hours racing in Mario Kart. Or, you can go old-school mode and pull out the Super Nintendo. Whatever you choose to play, spending one evening with video game will fill it with fun and laughter. Just make sure that there is no hard feeling. Play for fun because that is the purpose of video games, especially when there is more than one player.

Slumber Party

We all have those fond memories of having a slumber party at your friend's home. When you combine this idea with video games, you are reliving your childhood memory. It has been, what, more than ten years already since you have been to a slumber party. So, grab some blankets, pillows, your favorite movies, board games, snacks, etc. Put on your favorite and most comfy pajamas and hang out with your friends or family, playing and talking all night long.

Movie Marathon

This is a good activity to have if you want to have a slumber party. Pick your favorite movies or series, some musicals, or your favorite classic Disney movies, etc. Grab some popcorn, curl up on the couch with your pillow or wrap yourself in your blanket like a burrito and hit play.

Get Crafty

Maybe you come across an interesting Pinterest project or home DIY that you want to try out. Or maybe you have come across Bob Ross painting series (you should check it out) and you want to try it out. If so, why not have someone join in the activity? Maybe try to draw portraits of each other. If anything, everyone will have a good laugh.

Watch a Concert

If you love music but you want to save some money, then there are many fantastic recorded live concerts and documentaries on YouTube or other streaming platforms. You can spend the night binging or just put it in the background while you are doing other things and it still serves as a fun and different form of entertainment.

Play a Word Associated Game

Another way to spend an evening is by playing word games. Start by writing down several different words on different slips of paper. Then, have each participant take one slip and tell a story about the first thing that comes to their mind. This is a great way to learn more about one another. Don't know what to write, we have some ideas for you:

7th grade, proud, purple, ice cream, random, picture, roller coaster, bike, vacation, spring break, dog, create, laugh, swimming, friend, money, weather, 2, orange, road trip, first, camping, shopping, sing, ticket, gym, embarrassed, dream, zoo, and summer.

Play a Board Game or Card Game

This should be one of the things that instantly cross your mind when you think of how to spend your Fredagshygge night, for good reasons. They are very fun. Games like Scrabble, Yahtzee, Phase 10, Skip-Bo are some of the good games out there. If you are feeling adventurous, play Monopoly or Uno. Combine this with your concert or movie idea, or just playing your favorite tunes and you will have a beautiful evening.

Virtual Double Date

Do you have someone you live that you have not seen for quite a while? Maybe they live a few hours away from you or maybe they are in another part of the country. Heck, maybe you are in a long-distance relationship. Whatever the case may be, you can still connect with them, which is how technology should be used. Just open up FaceTime or Skype and have a virtual date! Team up with them on the interwebs and play games together. Pictionary or any games that you can think of is a great way to reconnect with someone that you have not seen in a while.

Have a Wine Tasting

You can also play the role of an expert wine taster and pick up a few different wines, a range of cheese and fruit, then do your own wine tasting right at home. That way, you know what kind of liquor suits your fancy. However, if you do not want to spend a fortune buying different bottles of wine, then go for the smaller-sized bottles. Many companies are now making them that can fill 1.5 to 3 glasses per bottle so you can try a large variety of wine without spending too much on it.

Hygge Music and Movies

Creating the right hygge atmosphere does not involve scents and scenery alone because it is the invisible energy, a state of mind where you feel connected, filled with proximity and shared values. You cannot observe it physically, but everyone can tell when that warm energy washes over them. In addition to the previous steps to create a hygge atmosphere, you can also use music to create the right atmosphere.

Hygge Music

Music is a way to combine a way of relaxing and enjoying life with your loved ones to create the perfect cozy and familiar atmosphere. Again, it all comes down to personal preference, but there are a few things you should look for.

First, the song should highlight intimacy by not being noisy and allowing you to feel close to the music. "Sometimes You Need" by Rufus Wainwright is a good example. Secondly, the song should have warmth. Here, "Everything in Its Right Place" by Radiohead is a perfect example. It is hard not to think of a fireplace when listening to it. There are many songs out there. We also recommend you check out Jazz Hop genre as the tempo is slow, perfect for a cozy atmosphere. Other songs include:

- Ain't No Sunshine from Sivuca
- What Are You Doing the Rest of Your Life from Bill Evans
- Lua, Lua, Lua, Lua from Gal Costa
- As She Walked Away from Brother Jack McDuff
- I'm Still in Love with You from Marcia Aitken
- Rio Para Trás from Celso
- The Sewing Machine from The Sea and Cake
- What Are You Doing the Rest of Your Life from Bill Evans
- Chicago from Surfjan Stevens
- I Saw the End from Ardency
- Alison from Swimming
- I wish You Love from Blossom Dearie
- When You Told Me from Bodebrixen
- Dear Santa from Mr Little Jeans
- Det'cember from Sys Bjerre
- It's Christmas from Cody
- Be Mine from Alice Boman
- Winter Song from Caesars
- Dreams Today from Efterklang
- Suppegjok from Lindstrom and Prins Thomas
- Water Flow from Klyne
- Tokka from Agnes Obel
- Samba Saravah from Pierre Barouh
- Mythological Beauty from Big Thief
- Just For Now from Cloud

- Tapes
- Love Like Ghosts from Lord Huron
- Angela from The Lumineers
- Ghosts from Laura Maling
- Control
- Pain from The War on Drugs
- Rebel Heart from First Aid Kit

Hygge Movies

In addition to music, you should also have a few movie ideas ready if you do wish to have a hygge evening in addition to your favorite movies. While some movies are great, they do not really fit the theme of hygge. So, consider the following as pointers to help you compile your hygge movie list and create the perfect atmosphere to enjoy those movies.

Heart-Warming Movies

Have a collection of love movies that just make you smile. Focus Features' recent release "Loving" that features Oscar nominee Ruth Negga and Joel Edgerton as Mildred and Richard Loving. If you want to embrace the Nordic spirit, consider watching "The Danish Girl", which was set in the art world of the good old 1920s. Being a bittersweet romantic tale, it conveys the importance of acceptance and unconditional love. If you want something lighthearted, try out "In Bruges", which is a drywittedcaper starring Colin Farrell and took place in the historic Belgian city.

Soft, Fuzzy Things

When you have found the movie you want to watch, it is time to think of your viewing spot. The best and quickest way to hygge up your place is by surrounding yourself with soft textures and comforting tones that soothe your eyes and your skin. Of course, no Scandinavian-inspired setup is complete without a bit of sheepskin. Of course, there is no need to go out of your way. Having one or two snuggle-able home accessories such as knit-covered pillows or faux fur throws and you are set.

To comfy yourself up further, put on something soft like cashmere robes, socks, slippers, or your own pajamas. Whatever suits you.

Lighting

You might see this coming, but we all know that candles are needed in anything hygge. Use scented candles if you can afford one, using one of the scents we discussed previously. Or, you can just light ordinary candles and use diffusers to get your scent. The idea is to provide soft lighting while you enjoy your movie. If you have a fireplace and it is particularly cold that night, then light that up.

Hygge

It is also worth pointing out that the light coming from your TV screen might strain your eyes, and candle lights or even fireplace lights will not cut it. Therefore, you should lower the brightness of your TV to match the light in the room so you can watch movies comfortable in for an extended period of time.

Warm Drinks

When you watch movies that just melts your heart, you might want to drink something equally hot to reflect your feelings. You can never go wrong with tea, but you can also try hot chocolate. If you watch movies in the evening, avoid caffeinated drinks because it will keep you awake at night.

Other Movies

Want more movies that give you an emotional and visual escape from your everyday life? Here are a few more movies to evoke feelings of wistful nostalgia that will carry out into a dreamy, fanciful time and place for a while.

The first two is "Anna of Green Gables", and "Anne of Green Gables; The Sequel" that are based on L.M. Montgomery's series. You might feel like it is a family reunion every time you watch it. We suggest you watch it around Christmas time.

The next two is "The Man from Snowy River", and "Return to Snowy River". Without spoiling everything, we follow a man called Jim Craig who was played by Tom Burlinson. Jim strives to keep his homestead after his father passed away in a tragic accident. He eventually falls in love with Jessica, who is the daughter of a belligerent wealthy landowner. It's worth pointing out that Tom Burlingson did an amazing job in portraying Jim Craig. This movie is a must-watch.

"Sarah, Plain and Tall" comes in the fifth on our list. We look at a woman who describes herself as "plain and tall", hailing from New England. She responds to an ad by a Midwestern widower who is looking for a bride to help him raise his two children. Again, not spoiling anything, but you should give it a shot.

"Love Comes Softly" is a movie that will grip your heart, while being inspiring at the same time. If you decide to watch this movie, make sure to have some tissues nearby, just in case.

"Little Women" is a sweet movie featuring cozy and charming wintery scenes, perfect for a hygge night.

If you want something more on the comedic side, then check out "The Holiday". It is a romantic comedy. Here, we get to see the adventure of a British woman and an American who switch homes during the holiday. Then, hilarity, truths, and charm ensue.

"Family Stone" also highlight the holiday spirit, but not in the classic way. It shows the modern day family life, highlighting the quirks, the challenges, and the changes. It is a charming, funny, and heart-melting film about family bonds during Christmas.

Hygge

Finally, you should have "It's a Wonderful Life" in your list. This is arguably one of the best movies to watch during Christmas. It is both inspirational and tear-jerking, so again have some tissues ready.

Alexandra Jessen

Hygge and Food

Now that we have talked about movies, music, and how to set up your home to be as hygge as possible, there is yet another thing we should address. We have talked extensively about eating your comfort food or cooking your favorite meals. While those will be enough, it never hurts to try something new, isn't it? In this section, we will look at some hygge dishes that you should try cooking at home.

Morning Porridge

Let us start with something very simple. To cook this dish, you will need:

- 250ml/1 cup of water
- 100g/3.5oz of fresh blueberries
- 125g/4.5oz of mixed flakes
- 40g/ 1/3 cup of almonds, chopped
- A pinch of salt
- Raisins
- Cold milk
- 1 apple, cored and diced

Then, simply put the water, blueberries, flakes, almonds, and apple in a small saucepan. Let them simmer for eight minutes and stir it frequently. Add salt and serve. Cold milk and raisins are optional.

Hygge

Winter Apple Layer Cake

This is your go-to cake other than chocolate cake. First, start working on the apple sauce, the layers, and the cream.

For the apple sauce, you need:

- 1 tbsp lemon juice
- 40g/ ¼ cup caster sugar (granulated)
- 600g/1lb/5oz Bramley apples

For the layers, you need:

- 2 tsp ground cardamom
- 3 tsp ground cinnamon
- 1 egg
- 175g/ ¾ cup of caster sugar (granulated)
- 175g/ ¾ cup minus 1 tsp soft butter
- 175g/ 1 1/3 cups of plain, all-purpose flour

For the cream, you need:

- 100ml/scant ½ cup of single, light cream
- 300ml/generous 1 ½ cups of double, heavy cream
- 100g/ 3 ½oz of hazelnuts

When you have everything ready, start by working on the apple sauce. Peel and dice the apples and put them into a pan along with the sugar and lemon juice. Let them simmer for about 15 to

20 minutes. Take it off the heat when you have a smooth sauce and set it aside to cool.

Next, preheat the oven to 200°C/400°F/gas mark 6. Then, draw a 20cm or 8in circle with a pencil on 7 sheets of baking parchment. Turn them over and arrange on as many baking sheets as needed to fit. Of course, you might need to bake them in batches.

From there, beat the butter and sugar together until it becomes fluffy before beating in the egg. Mix the spices and flour together and then fold it into the creamed mixture. Spread the mixture evenly using a spatula inside each visible circle on the baking parchment.

Then, bake in the oven for 6 to 8 minutes until the edges start to have some color. Finally, set it aside to cool on the sheets of baking parchment on a wire rack. Again, you might need to bake in batches.

While the layers are cooling, start roasting the hazelnuts. Spread them on a baking sheet and roast them in the oven before wrapping them in a clean towel and rub them until the skins come off. Then, chop them roughly. Then, whip both creams together with the icing sugar and stir in 2/3 of the chopped hazelnuts.

Finally, assemble the cake right before serving because it gets soft quickly. Put a crisp layer on a serving plate and add in some apple sauce, then another crisp layer and add in some cream.

Repeat this pattern twice before adding the last crisp layer with apple sauce on the top. Sprinkle the remaining chopped hazelnuts and serve.

Bagel Egg Kale Strata

This dish has a different color palette but it is delicious all the same. Here are the ingredients:

- 2 tbsp avocado oil
- 1 bunch dino kale, stems removed
- 10 large eggs
- 2 tsp and 1 teaspoon of kosher salt
- Scant teaspoon black pepper
- ½ cup of coconut milk
- ½ tsp of onion powder
- ½ large bunch of fresh dill, finely chopped
- 2 or 3 of everything bagels like Canyon Bakehouse
- 8oz of salt-cured pork belly, diced into 1/2in cubes
- Avocado spray to grease dishes

Start by setting a saucepan with water on high heat. When it is boiling, add 2 tsp of kosher salt and kale. Boil it from 5 to 7 minutes until the kale becomes wilted before draining. Finely chop the kale when it is cool enough to handle. Then, set it aside.

Next, use a small frying pan or wipe the saucepan dry before setting it on high heat again. Add cubed pork belly when the pan is hot, no oil is needed, and cook for a few minutes until the pork has golden brown sear. Strain it from grease and set ¾ of it aside for the egg mixture. Save the remaining to toss on top of each.

It is worth noting that when you use a stainless steel saucepan or skillet, the pork will stick at first. This is normal. It will release from the pan when seared.

Then, combine the eggs with 1 tsp of kosher salt, black pepper, coconut milk, and onion, and whisk. Split the bagels in half and make one-inch pieces to add to the egg mixture. From there, add chopped kale, oil, dill, and the ¾ of the pork bits. Toss egg mixture in to combine, and make sure all the ingredients are coated with egg.

Grease the crème brûlée dishes or casserole dish using spray baking dish before distributing the egg mixture evenly into the dishes or diss. If you have any remaining egg liquid, pour it into the crack and crevices.

For the remaining pork bits, spring a few pieces of pork over the dishes you prepared and cover them with aluminum foil. Put them into the fridge to refrigerate at least 2 hours, but it is best to leave it overnight.

When it is time to prepare, preheat the oven to 375°F. Then, prepare rimmed baking sheets lined with parchment paper so you can clean things up easier. Next, put the brûlée dishes or casserole dish on the baking sheet. Bake it for 20 minutes (covered with foil, of course). Then, uncover and continue to bake for another 7 to 10 minutes until the egg has set. Then, serve it hot or warm.

Nordic Tomato Soup with Rye

If you want to cook with a Nordic touch, this is the dish for you. You will need:

- 1 small bunch of parsley, chopped
- 1 onion, diced
- 1 carrot, peeled and diced
- 1 celery stalk, thinly sliced
- 2 bay leaves
- 2l/ 8 ½ cup of vegetable stock
- 2 tbsp of tomato purée (paste)
- 200g/7oz of rye grains
- 200g/7 of celeriac, peeled and diced
- 200ml/1 cup of white wine
- 3 400g cans or 3 cups of chopped tomatoes
- 3 garlic cloves, finely chopped

Start by rinsing the grains in cold water then drain. Place it in a saucepan and add cold water until the grains are covered. Cover the pan, bring it to boil, and let it simmer for 20 minutes. Drain and set it aside.

Move to large saucepan, sauté the onion, garlic, carrot, celeriac, and celery in the olive oil for 2 to 3 minutes. Add tomatoes, tomato purée, wine, bay leaves, and stock. Bring it to boil before letting it simmer (covered) for 10 minutes before adding the drained rye grains. Then, season to taste with salt and pepper. Serve immediately, sprinkled with parsley.

Cold Rice Puddings

Yet another great comfort food. Here are the things you will need:

- 2 vanilla pods (beans)
- 1.6l or 7 cups of whole milk
- 2 tsp sea salt
- 2 tbsp caster sugar (granulated)
- 300ml/ 1 ¼ cups of water
- 300g/ 1 2/3 cups of short-grain pudding rice
- 500ml/ 2 cups of double heavy cream

You also need to work on the cherry sauce:

- 3 tbsp of cornflour (cornstarch)
- 500ml/ 2 cups of water
- 1 vanilla pod (bean)
- 150g or ¾ cup of caster (granulated) sugar
- 700g or 1lb 9oz of pitted cherries, fresh or frozen

Hygge

Start by splitting one of the vanilla pods halfway, not cutting all the way through. Bring the water to boil in a large, heavy-based pan, and add the rice. Let it boil for 2 minutes while stirring. Then, add in the milk and split vanilla pod. Stir again until it returns to boil. Then, lower the heat, cover and cook for 15 to 20 minutes. Again, stir often so it doesn't catch. Continue to stir until the rice is just cooked. Then, remove from the heat, add salt, cover, and set aside for 10 minutes before stirring in the sugar. Leave until cold or overnight.

Next, remove the vanilla pod then transfer the cold rice mixture to a serving bowl. Set aside a whole almond, then chop the rest. Split the second vanilla pod halfway again, take out the seeds with the tip of your knife and put in the seed in the rice pudding. From there, whip the cream in a bowl until it forms soft peaks. Then, fold one-third of the cream into the rice to loosen, and fold in the rest before adding the chopped almonds. Then, taste the puddings for quality. It should be sweet with a touch of vanilla. Then, push the whole almond down into the pudding to hide it.

Moving on to the cherry sauce, start by mixing the cherries, sugar, vanilla pod and water in a saucepan. Bring it to boil before reducing the heat. Let it simmer for 15 minutes. From there, dust the cornflour into 2 tbsp water in a cup and stir. Add the cornflour paste slowly into the cherries, and stir it continuously until they become think. Then, add season to taste with sugar if you want.

Alexandra Jessen

Baked Camembert with Fresh Herbs

This is simple yet delicious. For this recipe, you will need:

- ½ baguette
- 1 package of Mons Camembert
- 3 tbsp of extra-virgin olive oil, divided
- 1 tsp of finely chopped fresh rosemary
- ½ tsp of fresh thyme leaves
- Assorted vegetables like carrot sticks, celery, endive, endive and/or sliced bell peppers

Start by cutting the baguette diagonally to produce long, thin slices. Brush both sides of the slices with 2 tablespoons of olive oil. Then, place the slices on a baking sheet before toasting them. Turn them once and leave them until both sides are golden brown, or for 15 minutes. Then, transfer them to a serving dish.

Next, lower the oven temperature to 350°F and line the baking sheet with parchment paper. Remove the cheese from the box and unwrap. Discard the wrapping. Then, carefully slice off the top layer of run and return cheese, cut side up, to the box. Then, drizzle with the remaining 1 tbsp of olive oil and sprinkle it with rosemary and thyme. From there, place the box of cheese on the baking sheet and bake it until it is hot and oozing. This should take between 15 to 20 minutes. Next, gently stir with a form to ensure that the cheese is melted all the way through. If not, continue to bake as needed.

When done, serve immediately with toasted baguette and vegetables.

Toasted Coconut Porridge

This is a simple coconut breakfast porridge, a cozy and wholesome breakfast. You will need:

- 1 14oz of canned coconut milk (either regular or light)
- ½ cup of quinoa
- 1 ½ cups of rolled oats
- 1 cup of juice or water
- ½ cup of unsweetened coconut flakes
- Cinnamon
- Salt
- Apply slices, peanut butter, or honey

Start by bringing the coconut milk to boil in a small saucepan. Then, add the quinoa and salt. Cook for 15 minutes, or until the quinoa is cooked. Then, add the juice or water, oats, cinnamon, and salt. Cook for a few more minutes until the oats soften up.

Then, put a nonstick skillet over medium-high heat, put in the coconut flakes and shake it in the pan until it is lightly toasted. Finally, serve up the porridge topped with toasted coconut or anything you want to put up there.

If you want a thicker porridge, add only half a cup of juice or water. If you want it softer, add the full cup. You can also start with half a cup and add more as the mixture soaks up the water. Also, you can use other seeds or grains. It is up to you to judge how much moisture and how much time each grain needs in order to cook.

Vegan Pumpkin Cinnamon Rolls

This is just as simple as it is healthy. You need to make the dough, filling, and topping separately. For the dough, you will need:

- 1 cup of unsweetened almond milk
- 1 packet of instant yeast (roughly 2 ¼ tsp)
- 1 tbsp of organic cane sugar
- ¼ tsp of sea salt
- ½ tsp of cinnamon
- 1 tsp of pumpkin pie spice
- 1/3 cup of pumpkin purée
- 2 tbsp of vegan butter
- 2 ¾ to 3 ¼ cups of unbleached, all-purpose flour

For the filling, you need:

- ½ cup of raw pecans (chopped)
- ½ tsp of pumpkin pie spice
- 1 tbsp of cinnamon

Hygge

- 1/3 cup of organic cane sugar
- ½ cup of pumpkin butter (optional)
- 2 ½ tbsp of vegan butter

For the topping, you need:

- ¼ cup of raw pecans (chopped)
- 1 tbsp of organic cane sugar
- 1 tbsp of pumpkin butter (optional)
- 2 tbsp of vegan butter

Now, let us start with the dough. Mix the almond milk and vegan butter in a small saucepan over medium heat or a large mixing bowl in the microwave every 30 seconds until the mixture is warm and melted, but not boiling. Then, remove the bowl or saucepan and let it cool for 110°F or 43°C or the temperature of bath water. It should be warm enough. Too hot and it will ruin the yeast. If you warm up the mixture on the stove, transfer the mixture to a large mixing bowl. Then, sprinkle on the yeast, salt, and sugar. Let active for 10 minutes before adding cinnamon, and pumpkin pie spice. Stir and let it sit for a few minutes before whisking in the pumpkin purée. Then, add in the flour, half a cup at a time, and stir as you go. The dough will become sticky. Lightly flour any surface and transfer the mixture when it is too thick to stir. Then, knead the mixture for a minute or until it forms a loose ball. Add flour as needed. Next, rinse your mixing bowl out and coat it with oil. Add the dough back and roll it around to coat it in oil. Cover the bowl with a plastic wrap and put it in a warm place for about an hour, or until the dough doubled in size. Then, flour any surface again and roll out the dough into a thin rectangle.

Next, work on the filling. Brush the dough with melted vegan and pumpkin butter, add sugar, pumpkin pie spice, sugar, cinnamon, and the pecans. Stir at one end and roll the dough up and situate seam side down. Then, cut the dough into 1.5 to 2-inch sections with a serrated knife or floss. Put the pieces into a well-greased 8x8 square or a pan of similar size.

Then, work on the topping. Brush the pieces with vegan butter mixed with pumpkin butter, then sprinkle in the cane sugar and pecans before covering them with plastic wrap. Set it on top of the oven to let rise again. Meanwhile, preheat the oven to 350°F or 176°C. Bake the rolls on the center rack for about 30 to 40 minutes when the oven is hot. Take out when the rolls are golden brown and crusty at the top. Let it cool for at least 10 minutes before serving.

Slow Cooker Creamy Tortellini Soup

This is pure comfort food, filled with vegetables, cheese tortellini, and Italian sausage. You will need:

- 1 cup of milk
- 5 cups of fresh baby spinach
- 12 oz packet three cheese tortellini

Hygge

- 36oz of evaporated milk
- ¼ cup of cornstarch, mixed and dissolved in ¼ cup of water
- 4 cups of beef broth
- ½ tsp salt
- 2 tsp beef bouillon powder
- 1 tbsp of Italian seasoning
- 4 cloves of garlic, minced
- 2 stalks of celery, chopped
- 2 large carrots, chopped
- 1 onion, chopped
- 1lb or 500g of ground Italian sausage

Start by placing the browned sausage, carrots, onion, celery, garlic, Italian seasoning, beef bouillon powder, salt, and broth in a 6-quart slow cooker bowl. Then, cover it and cook on high for 4 hours on low for 7 hours. After that, uncover and skim any fat on the top with a spoon. Discard it. Then, stir in the cornstarch mixture with the evaporated milk, add the tortellini, and mix well. Cover again and cook on high heat for 45 more minutes until the soup thickens and the tortellini is soft and cooked through. Then, add in the spinach, pressing the leaves down to submerge it completely in the liquid before covering again for 5 to 10 minutes until the leaves wilt. Next, pour in the milk, 1/3 cup at a time, as needed so to reach the desired thickness and consistency. Taste test and season it with salt and pepper if needed. Finally, serve it with crusty warmed bread.

Alexandra Jessen

It is worth pointing out that the Italian sausage gives the soup an amazing flavor, but you can always go for ground chicken, beef, or turkey sausage. If you don't like sausages, you can use plain ground meat. If you want a vegetarian variant, skip the meat. The soup thickens while it cools and it absorbs a lot of liquid along the way. So, you might need to add extra milk when you reheat leftovers so to maintain your desired level of creaminess.

Hygge and Self-Care

Hygge is so much more than just creating the right atmosphere and cozying up. The idea is to make you feel content, cozy, and satisfied. It is a lifestyle to soothe your soul after all of those long and stressful days at work. It is all about living in the moment, no matter how insignificant it is. It is giving yourself the chance to unwind by socializing with the ones you love. It is the joy of experiencing the simple things in life. In many ways, hygge is about self-care. As you might have guessed, hygge reduces your stress and makes you happier. That is why the Danes are among the happiest people on the planet. So, how do hygge ties in with self-care?

There are some key parts of hygge that are relevant to self-care. First, and most importantly, is being kind to yourself. All of us are guilty of treating ourselves badly and we sometimes do it simply because we hate ourselves. Slow down, stop, and treat yourself like how you would to someone you care about. Everyone has done something bad in their lives, and you cannot let your past define who you are. Take better care of yourselves. This brings us to the second element: comfort foods.

There is nothing better than eating something than what your grandmother used to cook. She made sure to keep your stomach stuffed and treated you very kindly, to the point that you were spoiled. Relive the memory and allow yourself to smile by cooking up your grandmother's dishes.

Sometimes, we just do not want to get out of the house. That is totally fine. We have talked extensively about the things you can do right at home. Actually, going out can be more tiring than fun to most people. Instead of a night out in heels, take off your shoes, kick back, and relax with a bottle of wine on the sofa by the fireplace. You can pamper yourself further by taking bubble baths and basically having a lot of "me time". So, here are some hygge ideas for self-care.

Be Your Own Best Friend

Loving yourself means that you no longer requiresupport from another person. Think of your social life as a platform held up by three pillars. One is friends and family, one is your significant other, and one is you. Without one of them, you might think that your life is unbalanced. While you can certainly lose your friends, family, and significant other, you can never lose yourself. Strengthen your relationship with yourself because,during the darkest moment, the only person you have is you.

Learn to be your biggest fan. If you make mistakes, do not beat yourself up too harshly for it. Never allow others to treat you poorly and believe that you are a good person who brings something good to the world.

While you're at it, try leading your life from your heart. It is true that the head is logical, but the heart makes you happy. You can never go wrong with a little bit of both, so let your heart guide you and put your best welfare first. Make decisions so you can achieve the future you desire.

Make Your Own Food

While this is often seen as a women's activity, there is no reason why men should not learn to cook. After all, self-love implies self-dependence. In reality, cooking is a very fun and rewarding activity. When you make your own recipe, you control what goes into your food. Remember that restaurants and fast food places do not really care about your health. They just want to make as much profit as they legally can, so they tend to use cheap, poor-quality ingredients or add too much salt to make their food taste better.

So, treat yourself to homemade meals when you can. Use fresh ingredients, and make sure to make them with a lot of love. Start with something very simple, like making sandwiches or bacon and egg. Then slowly work your way up.

On the topic of food, let us talk about water. Instead of buying a coke or diet coke (that doesn't work as well anyway), change to something that nourishes your body and soothe your soul. Earl Grey and green tea are some of the best things you can drink. If not, plain water works just fine. Actually, you should drink water as often as possible, not only during your hygge time. Drop the coke, and cut down on caffeine if possible. You can also try out lemon ginger tea, green lemonade, apple juice, and orange juice. After a long day, if you want to unwind, try some fine wine. Beers are often seen chucked down in one go. This is not hygge. Instead, take the time to savor the taste of red wine or scotch. If you had dome some wine tasting in a previous chapter, you should know what kind of wine you want. So, just have a glass nearby while you read your favorite book.

Education

Speaking of books, there are so many things to learn. You can take the time chilling in your hygge corner to continue studying. You can never know enough, after all, even after you obtained your Ph.D. Read while you relax, or listen to podcasts. This is a way of practicing your focus and mindfulness.

Vision Board

If you followed the 30-day challenge above, chances are that you have a gratitude journal and a list of things that make you happy. You can use those two as guides to create your vision board to guide your decisions in the future. In order to create the life you want, you need to keep your dreams at the top of your mind. This is one of the ways of practicing self-love – valuing your values and dreams.

Fewer and Better

We mentioned previously that minimalism is a part of hygge. Still, there is nothing stopping you from giving yourself an upgrade for some of the stuff you have. Instead of buying more, try to own fewer things but better quality. Make your investment count. Buy clothes that fit you properly (you will notice the difference). Are you satisfied with your bed and chair? If not, consider investing in ones that suit your taste. Make sure you are happy with your purchases. You can say that this is an indulgence, which is yet another element of hygge.

On the other end of the spectrum, you can always indulge in inexpensive things such as scented candles with your favorite scent. Sometimes, a box of chocolate is enough. Again, it is not really about the price or the number. It is how satisfied you are with the things that you have.

Conclusion

And that is about it. We would like to thank you for reading this far. You deserve a cookie. We hope that this book has been as useful as it is a joy to read. Remember, you do not need to follow every single step highlighted in this book, and there certainly are more ways to bring hygge into your life outside this book. Just remember the key elements of hygge such as coziness, togetherness, minimalism, carefree, and candles (of course). Being minimalist should be stressed because there is absolutely no reason to go out of your way to buy some extra stuff if you just want to get comfy, especially if it is expensive. Instead, get creative with the things you have and turn your home into a place where your heart truly is with hygge.

Finally, make sure to bring the hygge spirit to everyone, especially those you love. Sharing is caring, after all, and there is nothing better to share than this positive and relaxing energy that hygge produces.

Minimalism and Decluttering

Discover the secrets on How to live a meaningful life and Declutter your Home, Budget, Mind and Life with the Minimalist way of living

By

Alexandra Jessen

© **Copyright 2019 Alexandra Jessen, Minimalism and Decluttering - All rights reserved.**

In no way is it legal to reproduce, duplicate, or transmit any part of this document in either electronic means or in printed format. Recording of this publication is strictly prohibited and any storage of this document is not allowed unless with written permission from the author. All rights reserved.

Table of Contents

MINIMALISM 144

INTRODUCTION 146

DEFINITION OF MINIMALISM 148

HOW MINIMALISM IMPACTS PEOPLE 150

HOW CAN MINIMALISM CHANGE SOCIETY? 153

WAYS TO LIVE A HEALTHIER LIFESTYLE 155

THE KEY ASPECTS TO MINIMALISM 163

PRACTICAL WAYS TO SIMPLIFY YOUR LIFE 165

STEPS TO A MINIMALIST LIFESTYLE 172

SIMPLE WAYS TO SAVE MONEY 188

DIFFERENT LEVELS OF MINIMALISM 198

WHAT IS THE DOWNSIDE OF MINIMALISM? 201

THE MISTAKES OF MINIMALISM 204

CORE PRINCIPLES TO MAXIMIZE LIVING AND LIVE ON PURPOSE 213

SIMPLICITY OF MINDFULNESS AND MEDITATION 220

30-DAY MINIMALISM CHALLENGE 225

TIPS TO DECLUTTER YOUR HOME 231

DECLUTTERING: PRACTICAL STEPS FOR LIVING WITH LESS 233

TECHNIQUES FOR PRACTICAL DECLUTTERING 236

HOW TO START DECLUTTERING YOUR LIFE: 5 SIMPLE STEPS 240

HERE'S HOW TO MAKE MINIMALISM WORK FOR YOU 243

CONCLUSION 246

MINIMALISM

As someone who has tried absolutely everything in the pursuit of happiness and the peace we all long for, I realized it can't be found in the latest iPhone or the 100 room mansion, while these things can be amazing and fun, they won't lead to lasting happiness. But, even more than that is all the meaningless 'stuff' we have collected and consumed over the years actually weighs us down and with it drags down our mood and can make us feel heavy. One day, it simply became too much for me and I took a stand, I decided to declutter my house and get rid of anything that didn't serve a purpose or provide me with enjoyment, happiness or joy I decided to get rid of it. This didn't mean I got rid of all my possessions, instead it was the start of a life long journey towards basing my life on what I love and find meaningful.

I will never be someone who lives in a box with 3 possessions to their name, however, I have learned that living in a way that serves you and actually leaves you feeling fulfilled and happy in every moment. No longer am I trying to find myself through the constant objects how I used to. And, what I have decided to do is to share and help as many people live in a way that makes them as happy as they can be. There are no rules to this form of minimalism, everyone is different and that's what makes us human, but please approach all of these works by me as works that are only attempting to help you as much as I can from my own experience and years of research into what makes humans happy and joyful.

It's time we started focusing on what matters, and living life in a way that we love, that is meaningful and that fills us up with fulfillment, and I hope I can help you on your Journey.

ALEXANDRA JESSEN

All the best,

Alexandra

MINIMALISM AND DECLUTTERING

INTRODUCTION

If you're reading this eBook, chances are you're keen on decluttering and leaving on the adventure of a progressively minimalist lifestyle. Maybe this is your first enthusiastic, splendid peered toward attack into the universe of minimalism and you're searching for some basic tips to begin, or maybe you've figured out how to heave yourself back on the wagon after one more fizzled endeavor and are presently frantic for some motivation. Regardless of what your conditions, I am here to help with all the tips, traps and inspiration you need to set your minimalist objectives and stick to them!

Minimalism, like most other "- ism" developments, has unjustifiably turned into an object of criticism and, some of the time, by and large disdain, rejected as a hippy craze unlikely to stand the trial of time. Although these contentions may urge you to solidly walk out on minimalism (or run shouting for the slopes, if you're inclined to showy behavior), it's significant that numerous individuals harbor these feelings under the confused assumption that a noteworthy life change is basic to minimalism.

When we burrow a little more profound it turns out to be evident that, notwithstanding what you may have heard, minimalism just isn't tied in with living out of a cardboard box or segregating yourself from life's little pleasures or even quickly cutting back your 4 room cottage to a smallish lodge. Or maybe, the minimalist development essentially looks to perceive the overabundances of day by day life and prune them back to a progressively sensible dimension. In this sense, minimalism isn't tied in with denying ourselves, but rather about disposing of the extravagances we don't want so we have additional time and assets to focus on the things that really matter.

Removing clutter prepares for a life focused on the things that issue most. It opens up physical space in our home and mental space in our psyche. Living clutter free offers potential for more focus, more opportunity, passion and purposefulness. It diminishes pressure and money related commitments. Surprisingly better, expelling the physical clutter from our home establishes a foundation that makes significant life changes conceivable. It urges us to address assumptions and welcomes insightful thought of all aspects of our lives.

In this book, You will discover attentive and useful ideas on spring cleaning, dispersing your storeroom, and decluttering your psyche. This issue also addresses vital generational issues, for example, how to assist your maturing guardians in cutting back their homes and how to show youthful kids to declutter their rooms.

You don't need to be effectively carrying on with a Minimalist life to appreciate this book. This book is for any individual who's not totally content with their present life. Question is that being cheerful and investigates how to carry on with an important life. If you can peruse this book with a receptive outlook you might have the capacity to make a stride back and take stock of your present life, you may find that specific things you are doing or things that you possess are hindering your very own joy or opportunity.

MINIMALISM AND DECLUTTERING

DEFINITION OF MINIMALISM

Minimalism is a development in art, move, music, and so forth. Starting during the 1960s, in which just the simple designs, structures, forms, and so on are used, frequently redundantly, and the art's uniqueness is limited.

If you have chosen to live with less, you may have also considered about minimalism. Finding out about modern day minimalists and people, living less complex livesmay have you confused about what minimalism really is. How can all of these people be minimalists, when their lives are so dissimilar?

It is marked by clarity, reason, and purposefulness. At its focus, minimalism isthe purposeful advancement of the things we most value and the expulsion of everything that diverts us from it.It is life that powers purposely. Thus, it powers enhancements in all aspects of your life.

Toward the starting, you may characterize minimalism as wiping out your refuse cabinet. When you begin to unclutter, you quickly observe the advantages of living with less. This benefit may be something as simple as always being able to find that one thing you used to spend time looking for. As you start to enjoy the advantage, you search for tactics to live more simply. What begins as an outside voyage (giving things away, cutting the link), turns out to be extremely personal, purposeful and more important. You begin to consider "stuff" things as well as commitment, debt and stress. Then, you perceive how this "stuff" is hindering your LIFE and choose to roll out a greater improvement. It's now that minimalism becomes more about who you are, rather than what you have.

Just, minimalism is:

ALEXANDRA JESSEN

› Ultimate simplicity
› Working towards genuine freedom
› Redefining freedom
› Expecting and receiving change
› Living with less
› The reply to "that's it"
› Making time and space to find what is really significant
› Spending additional time with people who lift me up and lifting them right back

HOW MINIMALISM IMPACTS PEOPLE

Whether you consider minimalism to be a philosophy, a truth or a guiding principle, its effects depend completely on what you decide to pursue.

As indicated by Joshua Becker, a key idea pioneer of the present minimalism development, minimalism is the deliberate advancement of the things we most value and the removal of everything that distract us from it.

So if the thing we most value is to love life, accomplish our own and professional objectives, and go on the most epic vacation, that is the thing that minimalism will assist us with doing.

But if the thing we most value includes having our very own effect outside lives, at that point minimalism will allow us to do that.

Minimalism Asks Life's Most Important Question.

I think what I cherish most about minimalism is that it drives us to confront ourselves. No more holing up behind purchases, behind accomplishments, or behind busy ness. We need to make sense of the response to the questions, what really matters most to me. I love that minimalism doesn't answer that question for us; we need to.

Minimalism Cultivates Self-Control.
As we become more thoughtful about what is on our notorious plate– from the things in our homes to the responsibilities in our timetables to the things on our to-do list– we figure out how to lean far from the driving forces that

instigate the abundance in the first place. We start to shift from "What do I want at this moment?" to "What is the best decision here long haul?"

Minimalism Removes Petty Excuses.

At times, there are simply bustling seasons. Relatives might be in need; a chain of disastrous occasions may unfurl; we may get ourselves financially, emotionally, relationally or professionally overpowered.

But eventually, minimalism evacuates the negligible reasons why we can't accomplish those objectives we guarantee to have. Decluttering implies we never again have that "garage to clean" on a Saturday, and we can actually make it to our friend's child's birthday. Making more edge in our timetables implies we can't always say "I would, but I'm too busy."With excuses gone, we can concentrate on those practices that assistance us be our best selves.

Minimalism EncouragesIntentional Consumption.

People who are minimalists still create purchases– they simply make them even moreattentively, less rashly. At times, this implies spending practically nothing; different occasions this implies spending more to make purchase that have a positive (as opposed to negative) affect.

While the supply chain for huge numbers of our purchases is yet dark, we are ending up progressively mindful of the impact our purchases have on the world. For instance, fast fashion has been outed for its abusive (some of the time life compromising) influenceswomen and children in helplesscommunities.Minimalism allows us to be increasingly keen and compassionate in the manner in which we purchase necessities– from **food** and attires to toiletries and tools.

Minimalism Frees Up Time And Money.

People usually start to consider minimalist living when they conclude that they have more than they need, and that abundance is interfering with the life they want to live. Thus, the initial step usually includes disposing of stuff, and submitting not to purchase progressively extrain the future.

The naturaleffect is that money (that used to be spent on pointlessitems), as well as time (that used to be spent arranging or obtaining superfluous things), is currentlyfreed.The additional time and money on hand permits us to give more away; while minimalism will not really make us liberal, it will give us a superior reason to be.

Step by step instructions to begin: begin monitoring where your money is going – write it all. Toward the week's end, audit your list to perceive what was vital and what was not. Cut out those non-necessities!

Minimalism Is A Strong "No" For An Even Stronger "Yes".

There comes a moment that each minimalist gets herself alone with her needs. When we've said no to excessgoods and abundance activities, we get ourselves alone with our thoughts. What, then? We are compelled to choose what (or its identity) known to humankind that deserves our "yes".

I consider this is the moment that some world changer has to come to. This pivotal choice to express yes to that thing– that one thing we feel propelled to seek after, that trumps all else– is vital to having the effect we would like to make. Minimalism takes us to that moment, but bravery and belief (and community) enable us to step onward.When we havepermitted ourselves to oust the additional, we can say a wholehearted "yes" without thinking back.

I consider minimalism also draws out the best in humankind. It just takes a look at crazy Black Friday film to see that Western culture's cutting edge consumerist standardsare just playing wrong. Who cares if you have a 50-inch TV rather than a 30-inch set? Is it really worth prying things out of someone else's hands to make sure you can make a sparing? People were notborn to expend and end up caught in a cycle of purchasing stuff with expectations of hoisting their social status or filling an emotional gap.

ALEXANDRA JESSEN

HOW CAN MINIMALISM CHANGE SOCIETY?

Minimalism in Society

There is extraordinary power in the asking of these questions to actuallyredefine society.

At last, society and culture are what we as individual members make it. If every individual from our public asked these inquiries looking for more joyful lives, we would live in a different world. No doubt, this world would be significantly quieter, greater communityoriented, less harming to the environment, and, in particular, more joyful.

The proof for minimalism's things are clear: Every non-minimalist will start scrutinizing their assets, life activities, use of personal time, the experiences they want to make, and ability to contribute something useful. In actuality, minimalism has planted the seeds of progress. I realize it has influenced my life along these lines.

Even ifstrict minimalism does not spread that far, its message can resound with everybody, and I do mean everybody. It is an emphasis on living: Imagine a public strongly focused on the experiences that really matter.

The Power of Minimalism

Above all else, minimalism is a change in perspective. Its most prominent impact is urging individuals to think, see, and act toward another path: towards not so much realism, but rather more positive life experiences. Minimalism reclassifies the idea oflife, regular and overall. Society trains us to join our status and notoriety to the things we possess – luxury brands, the most recent devices, or the most

MINIMALISM AND DECLUTTERING

fashionable clothing. Minimalism instructs us to move far from this attitude.

The minimalist, like a researcher, asks,

> What does it mean to live?
> What are the fundamentals of an important life?
> Is that all we need to be cheerful?

It isan adventure looking for the fundamentals of living a cheerful and significant life. By removing clutter, concentrating on time and life experiences, the minimalist has couple of silly diversions to draw her into overconsumption and debt. It is an examination, one might say, to perceive what sort of lifestyle can realize the most bliss and importance. The ideal approach to begin, as all great science does, is with the fundamentals.

ALEXANDRA JESSEN

WAYS TO LIVE A HEALTHIER LIFESTYLE

Here are the absolute most significant ways minimalism has enhanced my life—and can enhance yours as well:

IDecluttered

The initial move toward a minimalist lifestyle is decluttering. What number of lipsticks and scents did I have? What number of CDs I never listened to? Pens, nail shines, shoes, outfits, designs… you get the image. My work area was cluttered with paper, note pads and office materials.

Having too much stuff has gotten under my skin. If you analyze how much moneyI'veexpended on all of it, you'll get a sum that will take your breath away. I would preferably not do that.

During the second day after I settled on the choice, I began the long, exhausting procedure of decluttering. I discarded the stuff and I was not even sad about the money I had spent on it. The time had come to settle on this drastic choice, so I could continue with a fresh start.

I saw that as I decluttered my environment, my psyche moved toward becoming clearer, too. I looked into a bit and found that other people felt a similar way. Minimalism can make you feel calmer.

Understand that minimalism is not just about materialism

Most people think minimalism implies disposing of stuff. While that is a decent initial step and the observable step, minimalism actually has to do with the advantages we experience once we are on the opposite side of de-cluttering, says Joshua Fields Millburn of The

MINIMALISM AND DECLUTTERING

Minimalists. Those advantages, he says, extend to numerous unforeseen areas of life, from health and funds to relations and emotions. Millburn's books, narrative film, and podcast, all created with accomplice Ryan Nicodemus, incorporate heaps of tips identified with those different areas. But, he says, they all attach back to this underlying philosophy: "Minimalism is the thing that gets us past the things, so we can make room for life's most significant things, which really aren't things at all."

I have moreintentionality in my life.

Minimalism, above everything else, gets more intentionalitythat is prominent our lives. At first, we became intentional in the possessions we owned and brought into our home. But we before long found the introduce of "advance the most vital by evacuating each diversion" held promise and opportunity in innumerable aspects of life.

Figure out your finances with a "Need-Want-Like List"

Before minimalism, Millburn had a six-figure compensation, a major house, luxurycars, and costly clothes—as well as six-figure debt. Moneywasn't inherently awful," he says. "The issue was the choices I was making with the assets I had. So for me, minimalism was an approach to recapture control of how I use those assets. Millburn discovered a system that could work for other people. Wanting to understand where his money was going, he sat down and recorded eachcost from his home loan to his morning espresso. He then put all those costs into three classifications: Needs (necessities like sanctuary and nourishment), Wants (things you appreciate that increase the value of your life), and Likes (hasty purchases, like another new match of shoes). Then I took activity. In the firstmonth, I disposed of 100 percent of my Likes, which was not as difficult as it appeared. In the second month, I disposed of 100 percent of my Wants. The third month I decreased my Needs by moving to a smaller place and attempting other cost-sparing measures like utilizing less power, which spared me another 50 percent for each month. Once Millburn prevailing about escaping debt, he allowed himself to re-join the Wants that implied the most to him over into his life. "I got undeniably more incentive from those things because I knew if I was including something back in, I was doing as such with goal.

I have additional time and money than ever before.

Life is comprised of limited assets—money, time, energy, space (just to give some examples). By diminishing the quantity of physical belongings we claimed and purchased, we discovered a large number of those limited assets more accessible than any time in recent memory.

Reevaluate your relations

Millburn's minimalist way to deal with connections may at first stable brutal, but he urges individuals to listen to him: "Nearly all that I bring into my life, regardless of whether it's an ownership or a relationship, I must have the capacity to leave immediately." Many individuals remain involved with companions, spouses, and colleagues out of a feeling of carelessness or dread of progress, he clarifies. But an eagerness to leave what's commonplace methods you just hold the relations that genuinely convey an incentive to your life. "It sounds like a mystery, but my eagerness to leave has fortified the bonds I have with the nearest individuals in my life because we're not tied by commitment. If we're seeing someone's because we want to be, and we make the best within recent memory together." He adds a sort of aphorism to help keep relations in context (however, it pauses for a moment to soak in): "You can't change the people around you, but you can change the people around you.

I contrast myself less and other people.

We waste so much time and energy contrasting our lives with others. There is not a single euphoria in sight there. Investing all of our energy considering what we don't claim, causes us to miss valuing the things we do possess. Examination makes us feel we are passing up something— despite the fact that there is euphoria directly before us.

MINIMALISM AND DECLUTTERING

Since discovering minimalism and craving less as opposed to additional, I contrast myself less and other individuals—in any event regarding physical belongings.

Feel Liberated
You think you have the things you purchase. You areoff base. When you have too a significant number of them,they have you. When you begin purchasing less stuff, you will feel free. This was one of the best exercises I learned since I settled on the choice.

I propose you complete a basic mental exercise today. After you declutter your space, sit in the live with your back straight and your eyes shut. Relax! Quiet yourself down. Envision how more straightforward your life will be when you have less stuff. Express this to yourself: "I don't need numerous things. Starting now and into the foreseeable future, I'll be getting just the things I need." Repeat this activity each and every day.

It took just a couple of days of this rehearsing this activity and I saw I never again was taking a gander at garments and different things to purchase on the web. It's like you're sending that message to your subliminal dimensions, and that is where the longing originates from.

I measure the estimation of work in all the more satisfying terms.
Work gets talked about in too numerous undesirable terms—both inside and outside minimalist circles. Inside minimalist circles, work can frequently be viewed as something to be stayed away from. I take a different perspective. Work is satisfying when found in the correct setting.

I have found shrouded gifts and passions.
Minimalism, I assume, does not change our abilities or aptitudes. But it opens up chance to seek after them in manners we hadn't envisioned previously. All the while, it might uncover shrouded gifts and passions we never knew existed. Composing, is the best precedent in my life.

When we beat the compulsion to waste our most limited assets basically overseeing and seeking after an ever increasing number of physical belongings, it's stunning what else we find we can do well. This fills much more passion for living (as I referenced previously).

Remain careful
Minimalists live intentionally. If there is something in your life that you don't love, change it! When I began my minimalist adventure, I was in an occupation and a relationship that didn't serve me. Inside a half year, I was out of both of those, and more joyful than I'd at any point been. I like to consider what my optimal life resembles, and then work toward that. Removing the things that aren't serving you are the initial step to making the life that you want. An activity that really encourages me is to record what a perfect day would look like for you in five years time. At that point move in the direction of that objective.

Found MyWeaknesses
Minimalism implies being focused on the most basic needs. I began eating straightforward nourishment, wearing basic garments and settling on basic choices. It wasn't that easy. My mind played nasty traps on me.

For what reason don't I purchase only one more paper on the web? I'll begin chipping away at my own articles next time.

This dress is so adorable. It's on markdown. I'll never get this cost when I need it.

When I began persuading myself to get something I didn't totally need, I was finding my shortcomings. For what reason am I so connected to these things I want to purchase? It is safe to say that they are really improving my life? If the appropriate response is no, then I don't get them!

MINIMALISM AND DECLUTTERING

I have left a case for my children they will always remember.

Throughout the previous ten years, I have displayed for my kids that individual effects are not the way to joy, that security is found in their character, and the quest for bliss runs a different street than most promotions will let you know. These are important life exercises I expectation will shape their choices far into what's to come.

Wound up Conscious about the Way I Spend Money

Planning is certifiably not a fun activity. All things considered, it's something we totally need to do when endeavoring to set aside somemoney and carry on with a minimalist life. When I'm focused on spending less, I know where my money is going.

Here's my recommendation to you: Try monitoring your vital costs. Make needs. Pay the bills first. Then, get the nourishment you need for the week. Keep things insignificant! Try not to get nourishment you will discard.

You'll understand you're sparing a great deal of money directly after you begin rehearsing this strategy. You'll monitor all your costs, so you'll know when some of them are a bit much.

I have developed in my confidence and otherworldliness.

I don't compose much about my own confidence and spirituality—it's simply not something I do (however it's not elusive if you're searching for it). But as I think back more than ten years of minimalism, I can't disregard the effect and impact that minimalism has had on my spirituality—not that it has transformed my trust, but rather it has surely conveyed new profundity to it. And for that, I am eternally thankful.

Outside minimalist circles, work is that thing you do to profit as conceivable to purchase as much stuff as conceivable. This too, is unfortunate and narrow minded. Work is our main thing to convey advantage to society and the general population around us. When we do our function admirably, everybody benefits. Minimalism has caused me to see work in another, additionally satisfying light.

I took back control of my own life.
While I didn't have any acquaintance with it at the time, my choice to claim less was eventually about reclaiming control. It was tied in with reclaiming a control I didn't understand I had surrendered. It was tied in with saying no to societal weight and social standards and settling on the choice to live individually terms. Minimalism gives that advantage to all who seek after it.

I have more passion for living.
A satisfied life is a passionate life. A life spent seeking after things that issue inhales energy and force into our days. It isn't difficult to get up toward the beginning of the day when you realize your days mean an option that is more prominent than yourself. Minimalism diverted my life's energy toward quest for more prominent significance than material belongings—and impelled more passion because of it.

It's Easy to Pair Outfits
What amount of time do you think Mark Zuckerberg spends attempting to make sense of what to wear? My estimate isno time. He spares his energy and time for progressively essential things. He presumably wears whatever he sees first in the storage room.

That is the excellence of a minimalistic lifestyle. I pick random things and they go superbly well together. I picked them in view of straightforwardness, so all hues and plans are correlative.

I have achieved things I never envisioned conceivable.

Ten years prior, I never would have envisioned my life would look today like it actually does. This blog is perused by 1 million different people each and every month. I've composed books—with another one turning out soon. I

MINIMALISM AND DECLUTTERING

began a magazine and established a charitable association changing vagrant consideration around the globe. I've talked all over the world. And I've been met for papers and radio shows and podcasts. All the more imperatively, I have been increasingly occupied with my children's lives and marriage than at any other time.

ALEXANDRA JESSEN

THE KEY ASPECTS TO

MINIMALISM

While a minimalistic life will appear to be unique from one individual to the next, there are sure core values you should use to begin. You should concentrate on three things: expelling needless things, sustaining the basics, and making the most of your activities.

Evacuating needless things
As referenced above, evacuating needless things doesn't equivalent to precluding everything or discarding your assets. The attention is on the word 'needless' and the definition you apply to this word. You need to identify the things and activities in your life, which you need and value.

In minimalism, you want to impartially take a gander at every thing and think about its actual importance and incentive to you. To some it may mean expelling assets, for example, extravagant furnishings or scaling back to a smaller condo, while others may concentrate on decreasing their closet or shoe gathering.

Identifying needless things probably won't be as easy as it sounds. We will in general place a great deal of wistful incentive to things, as well as consider thefuture conceivable outcomes. For instance, it's easy to take a gander at your bread creator and persuade yourself you may need it later on. The key is to identify the reasons you value the specific thing and understand whether youactuallyneed it.

Notice that having less doesn't mean you can't have things or even add new things to your life. It's just about identifying the things you actually require and which add to your overall satisfaction.

MINIMALISM AND DECLUTTERING

Supporting the basics

Minimalism's basic standards also incorporate supporting the fundamentals. These naturally incorporate life's necessities, for example, nourishment, water and safe house. But you'll also have different fundamentals essential to yourself.

By making a note of the things that have the greatest effect on your bliss and prosperity, you can begin sustaining these aspects of your life more. You'll in all probability also identify the needless aspects of your assets and activities.

Make sure to take a gander at the above inquiries through both your private and work life. Minimalism isn't just about carrying on with a minimalistic lifestyle at home in your private space, but also about identifying the fundamentals in your vocation.

Making the most of your activities

The last rule manages making the most of your activities. You want to begin evading things that don't make a difference to you or add to your prosperity and satisfaction.

Each move you make and each purchase you make ought to have a significance behind it. These activities ought to positively affect your life.

Making the most of your activities is to a great extent about supportability as well. It's not just about the momentary effect or joy, but the long haul affect.

Another vehicle may satisfy you for multi month, but following a year, you may be tired of seeing it.

Rather than searching for the transient reward and effect, you want to discover the things and activities that keep on having an impact long into what's to come.

ALEXANDRA JESSEN

PRACTICAL WAYS TO SIMPLIFY YOUR LIFE

Decide Your Vision

As with anything new you acquaint into your life pointed with change or better it, you need to realize what you're attempting to accomplish.

This could be characterized as finding your why.

The vision may be as basic as decluttering your home and pressing lighter when voyaging or as comprehensive as a shifting your whole lifestyle or scaling back your habitation. The fact of the matter is you have a dream at the top of the priority list and base your choices around it.

Asking yourself the why, what, how, when and who can help steer you the correct way.

› Why would you like to bring components of minimalism into your life?
› What benefits would you say you are endeavoring to get?
› How does the perfect state look when you picture it?
› When would you like to begin and to what extent will it take to achieve that state?
› Who else will be a piece of this procedure and shift?

For me, the vision is only simplification by decreasing clutter (physically and mentally) so as to save my time and energy to concentrate more on what conveys an incentive to my life.

MINIMALISM AND DECLUTTERING

Work On Being Paper Free

To proceed with the computerized cleaning topic above, getting to be sans paper as most ideal is an open door given on account of the advanced world.

Regardless of whether it's magazines, papers, books, charges, reports for work or other mail and paper products, it's truly easy to fill space around the home and office.

Nonetheless, the vast majority of those have a computerized answer for help limit the physical clutter.

> › Kindle (or other tablet) to house your books and magazines
> › Turning all bills, articulations and key correspondence to email over paper mail
> › Schedule paper cleanses, like our minimalism review, to help keep it a need
> › Digitize your archives with photographs on your telephone or tablet and then spare them digitally
> › Encourage collaborators to print less records and be a pioneer in that space
> › Rethink how much paper towel, napkins and bathroom tissue you're utilizing

The hardest piece of this paper free attitude for me is certainly the books.

I've constantly cherished adding new books to the rack. Regardless of whether it's the discussions they can begin, the chance to loan to other people or only an inborn accumulating attitude, this will be the hardest of the minimalism tips for me to completely actualize.

Complete A Minimalism Audit

So as to begin the change and shift your lifestyle, it's useful to realize what you're managing in general.

Enter the minimalism review.

This could incorporate a review of possibly either of the physical merchandise and the psychological side of what's creation your life progressively mind boggling or muddled.

The key is it's associated with your vision above and what YOU want.

Potential areas to consider with your review:

> Home
> Office
> Car
> Subscriptions and Services
> Digital Activity
> Habits
> Thoughts
> Tasks

Basically, if you're hoping to simplify your life you need to think about all aspects of it. Review your present circumstance to best understand the open doors accessible to achieve your objectives.

Another strategy to help reviewing your life is to play out a period track of all that you do from the minute you wake up until the point that you hit the hay.

Toggl is an administration that encourages you do only that with their straightforward (yet ground-breaking) time following application. Toggl gives you a comprehensive understanding of where your time is being gone through with their detailing highlights. It's a paid stage but they offer a free multi day preliminary.

Begin Small

In indistinguishable vein from another eating routine or wellness schedule, it's generally best practice to begin moderate with your minimalism outlook.

Making a plunge head initially can be compelling and fast-track the achievement you're attempting to accomplish. Be that as it may, it can also prompt errors or getting wore out.

The last thing you want to do is move all that you claim or change too much and understand this wasn't the lifestyle you wanted.

› Pick one propensity to actualize that underpins your vision
› Fill one tote sack of garments to give
› Alter a couple of components of your day by day schedule
› Start with one room in your house

Small successes, make energy.

Pick one spotlight territory previously based on your vision and starting review. Begin small and master that before moving onto the following need or opportunity.

Swing Clutter To Money

As far as the physical side of minimalism, a frequently ignored profit by actualizing some minimalism into your life is turning your clutter to money.

When I chose to put taking control of my money and life as a best need, one of the primary easy money related successes I had immediately was moving $1,800 worth of "stuff".

These were things that aggregated in my capacity unit, in the storage room, under the bed, on the rack, and so on over forever and a day of amassing. They were once in a while, if regularly, being used or giving any an incentive to my life.

A large portion of the people I converse with have had a comparative experience or store of "stuff" developed.

Regardless of whether it's a one-time scrub to begin simplifying your life that at that point turns into a yearly review, turn that clutter to money and use those assets towards your money related objectives.

Decluttr

Decluttr is a free application and site that allows you to turn the "stuff" you've collected into money. It's strength is electronic, tech things, computer games, DVDs, and so forth and even lego.

You just output the scanner tag (ISBN) of the thing with the Decluttr application and Decluttr gives you a quick offer.

They then send you a prepaid delivery name and settle your installments after they've gotten your things. No closeouts, no expenses and an easy to use application (or web) stage. Additionally you can get to free sending and protection inclusion on your things.

Be Honest and Embrace It

A standout amongst the best minimalism tips I've taken from different web journals, podcasts and content regarding the matter is to be straightforward.

Especially when you're simply beginning to endeavor to simplify your life.

This applies at as high of a dimension as your overall vision with minimalism and down to the granular dimension of "do I really need this coat?".

Regardless of whether you simply want a cleaner, progressively sorted out front room or to scale back your SUV, genuineness will assume a key job.

Given the potential changes coming could be a drastic shift, you will want to grasp it. What preferable approach to do that over gain from others and associate with other seeking after a minimalist, more straightforward lifestyle.

There are a huge number of individuals web based looking to declutter, simplify, expel pressure and carry on with a progressively healthy lifestyle.

Be straightforward, grasp it and associate.

Play out A Digital Cleaning

Decluttering doesn't need to just incorporate the physical materials you forces. The computerized world we as a whole regular so frequently gives various basic approaches to bring minimalism into your life too.

What areas of your online propensities and cell phone utilization actually convey value? Which are additional time and mind wasters than helpful? Would you be able to simplify the advanced world's job in your life?

MINIMALISM AND DECLUTTERING

Some prevalent arrangements depending your circumstance may include:

> › Reduce email memberships
> › Limit program tabs open
> › Keep a negligible number of bookmarks
> › Set a specific time for browsing email
> › Disconnect from gadgets at select occasions
> › Delete pointless applications from your telephone

Contingent upon your profession, family and living circumstance certain things won't be feasible You need to discover what works and advantages you.

Keep in mind It's More Than Just Physical Items

The principal thing that frequently strikes a chord for some (counting myself) when you consider minimalism is likely a cutting edge flat with constrained furnishings. Most likely white walls, two seats, small table, one encircled picture and a plant.

That is clearly a speculation.

It's a mentality, change in lifestyle, shift in propensities, new viewpoint and a great deal more. There can be ecological, financial, social and emotional wellness benefits.

It tends to be anything YOU desire it to be.

Separating of superfluous physical things to decrease clutter is obviously part of the condition but it's something other than that.

Value Experiences Over Materials

A typical amateur minimalism tip is to value experiences over materials. Use the assets you have, regardless of whether it's time or money, to appreciate "living" over gathering.

In the realm of simplifying your life, valueing experiences over materials can have various advantages – for your psyche, wallet, lifestyle, health and more.

Manufacture new abilities by taking courses and classes.

ALEXANDRA JESSEN

Sort out experiences for you, your family, companions and friends and family.

Possibly it's a parity of experiences and things. Possibly it's vigorously tilted to experiences. You need to ask yourself what conveys more an incentive to your life.

MINIMALISM AND DECLUTTERING

STEPS TO A

MINIMALIST LIFESTYLE

When you've met the choice to carry on with an increasingly oversimplified life, you'll be defied with the inquiry how you will approach this gigantic task. You want to simplify your life, but the multifaceted nature of the task is terrifying. There are such a large number of things that aggregated during the time that you don't realize where in any case. In the meantime, such a significant number of difficult inquiries need to be tended to. Limiting essentially can feel in these circumstances too enormous of a challenge. The sheer size of the minimalism challenge can be very overpowering, especially before all else.

But stress not. You don't need to minimalize your whole life from one day to the next. While there are extraordinary cases of people who dispose of all that they have starting with one day then onto the next, this may not really be the best alternative for you. When it comes to minimalism, it's critical to just simply begin. It's not all that imperative to achieve the goal (for example a minimalist lifestyle) promptly. Rather, minimalism is a voyage. Make small strides and begin completing one thing after another. Dispose of one superfluous belonging at any given moment. Kill one diverting movement after another. Along these lines you will make the progress to a minimalist life much smoother.

The basic thought and procedure of minimalism can be abridged in two stages. The initial step comprises of identifying what is vital and significant to you. The second step comprises of disposing of basically everything that isn't fundamental and does not increase the value of your life. As easy as this sounds, this can be a significant complex process. Consequently, it's useful to part the whole procedure of limiting your life into easier advances that can be tended to in a steady progression.

Here are the fundamental advances you can take to simplify your life and to live more minimalistic.

Assess your life.

Set needs. At the foundation of turning into a minimalist lies an examination of your life. It's the first and maybe most essential advance towards simplifying your life. Indeed, this progression is important to the point that it must not be ignored. What you want to do During this assessment of your life is to identify what's most significant and essential to you. Discover what components of your life include the bestvalue, satisfaction and importance to your life. Doing as such will assist you with settingyour needs straight. With an unmistakable understanding of what's really imperative to you, it's a lot easier to start the way toward limiting. Organizing encourages you to understand the advantages of making room in your life for the fundamental. Without this sort of understanding, you probably won't feel all too OK with disposing of insignificant things you've become used to. For example, if you try to quit staring at the TV, you may have a difficult time when you don't know absolutely for what reason you're doing it for. Be that as it may, if you understand that you surrender TV to have more opportunity to go through with a movement that really satisfies you, you'll be bound to oversee things. You can begin assessing your life by making a short rundown. Record the most essential things in your life and focus on these first. Concentrate on gradually making more space in your life for your needs.

Declutter

Regardless of whether you see it or not, clutter has a tremendous impact on your life. If you're in the propensity for shopping on the web when you feel exhausted or worried, you likely have heaps of clutter — things you may not focus on, garments you never wear, books you'll never peruse and contraptions you never again use. You don't need to consume all your common belongings to be a minimalist, but you should make a move if you have heaps of clutter in your home, office or elsewhere in your life.

Begin small. Consume it space by room, storeroom by wardrobe and cabinet by cabinet, until the point that you can sift through your effects and choose what needs to remain and what can go. You will feel a load lifting off your shoulders as your breathing room expands. Physical clutter will just divert you, so center your time and energy around controlling this aspect of your life. It will no uncertainty require investment to get yourself into the best possible attitude where you automatically stop and think before you purchase things. But up to that point, this is a begin.

Another approach to keep your life decluttered is to live in a smaller space. Small homes have picked up in prominence of late as an option in contrast to bigger flats, apartment suites or homes with superfluous space. If you have a smaller living space, you won't have space to store things you needn't bother with. Decreasing the measure of your living space can also be unfathomably financially savvy, as well as more eco-accommodating. While there are numerous advantages to owning a little home, making it easier to carrying on with a minimalist lifestyle is one of the best ones.

Choose One Clutter-Free Zone
Endeavoring to declutter your house is most likely too much. I unquestionably wouldn't prescribe doing it the manner in which I did!

Rather, name one space to be your without clutter zone. That could be your room, your lounge room, your carport – any room you feel could profit by de-cluttering the most.

Put aside an end of the week to really concentrate on making this room your aggregate sans clutter zone – look at my advisers for decluttering here for a few tips and exhortation! Having one room gotten out is also an incredible method to test whether you really want to wind up a minimalist and what amount having a without clutter space benefits you.

Do some exploration.

If you're perusing this at that point you're on the initial step to carrying on with a magnificent minimalist life. While many individuals may have found out about it, there are a great deal of confusions associated with minimalism. It is therefore reasonable to initially understand what the lifestyle is all about.

Sites, for example, theminimalist.com offer great rules into how to leave the lifestyle and notwithstanding refering to other people who are carrying on with the lifestyle. At the end of the day, learn as much as you can about the lifestyle and guarantee you are clear of all the misinterpretations.

Assess your assets.

After you've set your needs, it's an ideal opportunity to address your material belongings. Consider all that you claim and see whether these things line up with your needs. Investigate every possibility and question everything. Make sense of if the things you possess increase the value of your life or if they just occupy you and make mental commotion. It's regularly difficult to concede, but the assessment of your assets may feature that you possess very numerous things of next to zero value. These assets might be extravagant or engaging "pleasant to-have's," but where it counts ourselves we realize that they don't include any significant importance or reason to our lives. All they do is waste our time, deplete our energy or void our financial balances. Accumulate a rundown with all your assets that are repetitive and no longer of significant worth to you. Begin moderate by disposing of a couple of these things every week.

Unplug Once in a While

Try not to be reluctant to unplug yourself from your gadgets now and then so you can concentrate on different things occurring in the present. Truly, online networking can be addictive and come as a second nature, but it's essentialto eliminate your use. It's also undesirable to always come close yourself to other people, which is our main thing, regardless of whether we like to let it be known or not.

Studies demonstrate a few people check their gadgets each 6.5 minutes. Try not to be that individual. Enhance your in-person associations with individuals for an all the more compensating experience.

Relish the here and now — what's going on in your life minute by minute. If you're continually seeing the world through your telephone screen or by concentrating on what you don't have or aren't doing, it's a lot harder to gain experiences and investigate new things. Consider it. If you go to a show and take pictures and recordings the whole time, you'll miss a great deal of aspects of the experience. Be available, be careful and live at the time.

Keep in mind, toning it down would be ideal. You don't need to surrender all the material things you appreciate — you simply want to have a sheltered harmony between those things and what is realistically vital in your life. Concentrate less on your assets, and more on your overall joy.

Assess how you invest your energy.
Turning into a minimalist isn't just about de-cluttering physical items, but also about disposing of time-wasting exercises. The third step is therefore all about making sense of how you invest vast parts of your energy. Ask yourself the inquiry if the exercises you participate in increase the value of your life. Doing as such will assist you with spending less time with inefficient or even time-wasting exercises. This thusly will give you the opportunity of possessing more energy for the exercises you really appreciate. Take a gander at all that you do and each movement you consistently take part in. Record how much time you go through with pretty much purposeless exercises. See whether there are exercises that include positively no value. Identify if your responsibilities are in accordance with your

needs. When you have a decent understanding on how you invest your energy, check whether you can decrease unbeneficial exercises. Begin moderate by tending to the most problems that need to be addressed, each one in turn. It's smarter to free your life for the last time of one negative action than attempting to battle a few ones indifferently.

Diminish the bang.

When you've checked what you have, you would then be able to get to the useless stuff and dispose of it. Minimalism is basically about living with what you just need. For instance, you really needn't bother with a vehicle if open transportcould fill in as an adequate elective methods. Taking out the pointless things from your life decreases both the waste and the psychological exertion that sorting out those things go up against you.

Assess who you invest your energy with.

The general population you invest the vast majority of your energy with have an extraordinary impact upon your life. It's therefore just coherent that you want to support associations with constructive and empowering individuals. In the meantime, minimalism is tied in with identifying people who are nothing else except for lethal. Identify the people who deplete your energy and waste your time. Begin by investing less energy with the individuals who do only drag you down and demoralize you from seeking after your fantasies.

Set points of confinement.

When turning into a minimalist, you will find that there are sure exercises/things you just can't or don't want to dispose of. We as a whole have exercises we do frequently and can't manage without. You may need your telephone to make essential business calls. You may need your PC and web access to compose messages and to remain educated. So also, you may at present be keen on perusing rousing RSS channels or tuning in to motivating podcasts. The way to all these exercises is to set proper points of confinement. Try not to give these exercises a chance to meddle with your life. Try not to give them a chance to interfere with your work process. Rather, center around participating in these exercises just amid specified occasions. Set clear points of confinement to the recurrence you browse your messages – twice day by day is all that anyone could need. Set points of confinement for all that you routinely take part in. It will assist you with being increasingly gainful and focused.

Dispose Of Stuff And Be Clutter Free

The decluttering procedure is the easiest method to kick begin your adventure to minimalism. Doing this gradually and in a couple of scopes is by all accounts the most productive. I did around three or four ranges of decluttering before I was totally happy with all that I disposed of, and all that I kept. When you experience the decluttering procedure at a reasonable pace (for instance, don't do it all in one day or even in multi month), the change will be somewhat easier.

If you go from a full house to a for the most part void house medium-term, it will be an a lot harder change. It functioned admirably for me to attempt to hit around 5 areas for every week – and I picked small areas, like one work area cabinet or simply the sweaters in my storage room. Numerous individuals like to declutter by the room, so if that works for you begin there. In spite of the fact that it takes more time to declutter gradually, it is a lot easier to keep up a minimalist lifestyle if the decluttering procedure is done gradually and cautiously.

Choose what's critical.

You need to identify just things with genuine incentive to you. A ton of garbage that we keep can be credited to 'simply in case I need this' but I very uncertainty that you will need that vacant ramen bowl you've been importance to work into a DIY foot stool installation for the past 8 months. If you can't locate a fair use for a thing, dispose of it.

Dispose of the abundance.
Over disposing of the pointless, one ought to also dispose of the overabundance. For example, you don't really need numerous pots and skillet nor do your pets need such a significant number of beds. Abundance just uses up space that you could commit to something increasingly critical or leave unfilled. There is no need to fill each alcove and corner with a thing from your movements or some other kind of things that just serves to draw the eye. The objective ought to be to have all your assets fill a need and be utilitarian.

Get objectives.
Minimalism is predominantly a tool to accomplish a more joyful lifestyle. Therefore, to start carrying on with a minimalist lifestyle, it implies you should have an objective. This can be anything from decreasing heading out or over the top spending to better your vocation or meet your own objectives.

Lift Productivity With Minimalist Work Habits
We invest a great deal of energy at work, so it's critical to have a minimalist home as well as a minimalist office. Taking command over all aspects of your life will prompt less pressure, better time the executives, increased pay, and a superior work life balance.

The greatest increases in my pay and satisfaction with my work all originated from being purposeful in my life. When I settled on the life I wanted I was ready to leave my old corporate activity and begin my very own business, profiting that I at any point longed for. Building great propensities is a lot easier as a minimalist because we complete one critical thing that the vast majority don't do: we took an opportunity to understand what's vital to use and rolled out purposeful improvements to carry on with a superior life. That puts us route in front of the vast majority and the prizes are found in our own lives and in our profession.

MINIMALISM AND DECLUTTERING

Quit rationalizing.
A minimalist lifestyle has drawbacks. It requires enough self-control and genuineness to dissect things that offer no an incentive past a simply tasteful one. Extravagances and different overabundances are to be stayed away from if they don't help fill a need. This can turn out to be a challenge especially for an individual who is brimming with excuses.

Shop just for basics.

Minimalism doesn't mean you quit looking for products and enterprises. It keeps up on looking for basics. This is so as to guarantee that they don't waste assets on the pointless. The aftereffect of this is the general population wind up focusing their endeavors just on vital undertakings adapted towards them accomplishing their objectives.

Simplify Your Diet For Simple Meals
A straightforward eating regimen doesn't mean a bland eating routine or having a similar thing again and again. I initially begun by understanding my kitchen clutter and making sense of what I really need in my kitchen. When I thinned down the key fundamentals I discovered I delighted in cooking more, I currently anticipate getting back home and planning new dishes for all my suppers. Having an all around supplied, but simplified wash room helped a great deal towards this.

Like everything with minimalism, it's critical to make sense of what is ideal for you and streamline things keeping that in mind. A few people have an amazingly basic eating regimen of rice and beans, others discover a plant based eating routine or minimalist crude vegetarian diet to be appropriate for them. For me I begin with my most loved dishes and deciding a base arrangement of fixings that I generally keep on hand.

Quit storing.
Gathering pointless things eats into the space saved for things that could more readily serve the person. To battle this, it is essential to keep away from the gathering of

pointless things. Also, give things that are not needed to the individuals who might be ideally serviced by them.

Make arrangements.
The most ideal approach to accomplish objectives is to guarantee that there are plans set up for accomplishing the objectives. Plans are especially critical to new minimalists as they have more reality with the appropriation of this new lifestyle. Making arrangements puts the person in the best position to accomplish his objectives and make use of the assets that minimalism gives.

Travel delicately.
Each time you take an adventure, simply convey a couple of things to limit stuff and wastage. Voyaging delicately guarantees you just move around with fundamental things and nothing more. For example, you can pack just a large portion of the garments you need.

Grasp multipurpose tools.
Rather than utilizing numerous tools that all fill different needs, why not have a solitary tool that fills a huge number of needs. This is the advantage that minimalists are urged to search for in all their things. Multipurpose tools ration the space that could have been used up by having numerous tools to accomplish a similar objective. Why by a screw driver and a corkscrew while the Swiss Army Knife accompanies the two tools in a smaller plan.

Simplify Your Diet For Simple Meals
A basic eating regimen doesn't mean a bland eating regimen or having a similar thing again and again. I originally begun by understanding my kitchen clutter and making sense of what I really need in my kitchen. When I thinned down the key basics I discovered I delighted in cooking more, I currently anticipate getting back home and planning crisp dishes for all my suppers. Having a very much loaded, but simplified wash room helped a ton towards this.

Like everything with minimalism, it's essential to make sense of what is ideal for you and streamline things

MINIMALISM AND DECLUTTERING

keepingthat in mind. A few people have an incredibly straightforward eating routine of rice and beans, others discover a plant based eating regimen or minimalist crude vegetarian diet to be appropriate for them. For me I begin with my most loved dishes and deciding a base arrangement of fixings that I generally keep on hand.

Less internet based life is an or more.

Diminishing clutter in a minimalist's life also implies decreasing the measure of time wasted in devouring non-accommodating data. While internet based life can be an amazing asset for correspondence and business, it generally fills in as a stage for people to share vain and generally non-supportive titbits about their lives that you as a minimalist will have no use for. Web based life also urges spending because of innumerable customer focused on Ads.

Digitize everything.

Books and papers can be lumbering and space devouring. Be that as it may, advanced configurations for information and data can sit in your multipurpose tool and allow you hold an a lot bigger clump when contrasted with real physical content. It helps if you begin getting as much computerized substance as you can. digital books, online papers, music downloads rather than CDs, all these assistance guarantee that you don't fill your own space with pointless clutter.

Obtain whatever you don't need to purchase.

While it might be decent to possess you claim things, minimalists are urged to rather get things that they would use as opposed to getting them. This decreases the quantity of assets they have and guarantees they don't pile on clutter or store things. As long as you keep the obtained things safe and the loan specialist wouldn't fret sharing, like to acquire things as opposed to getting them.

Continuously pick quality over amount.

This is for the basic truth that quality things last longer than shabby options. Whenever you choose to purchase a thing, get one with the most elevated quality accessible. It will last you longer and guarantee that you do need to continue supplanting it and heaping up trash.

Financial plan your time.
Similarly as you spending plan your assets, spending plan your time. Guarantee that all the things you try to do are equipped towards edifying you. Try not to get things done for the only for it but appreciate whatever time you spend accomplishing something.

Representative as much as conceivable.
As frequently as conceivable, value your time and guarantee that all tasks that can be executed by another person are given to another person. This is in order to give the minimalist more opportunity to execute the tasks increasingly critical to them or those that the minimalist is better prepared to perform.

Before getting a thing, dispose of another.
One great principle guideline for the minimalist is to guarantee that before influencing a purchase of something, to dispose of any things officially claimed. This secures against clutter and the handling too numerous things.

Dispose of emotional clutter.
Similarly as the physical clutter can eat into physical space, emotional clutter can eat up mental space. In an offer to carry on with a minimalist lifestyle, evade emotional things and rather find sound outlets to guarantee your psychological state mirrors your physical space.

Separate an incentive from material things.
In turning into a decent minimalist, one needs to quit setting too much an incentive on material belongings. This is just feasible by setting significance on fundamental materials.

Eat straightforward and solid sustenances.
The minimalist lifestyle stretches out to dietary patterns. One ought to eat nourishments that meet sustenance

standards and make an effort not to over enjoy pointlessly costly nourishments. The sustenances ought to also be basic enough to get ready.

Choose to carry on with a superior life.
The general purpose of minimalist living is to encourage more joyful, progressively fulfilled living. The minimalist needs to chip away at doing precisely this by grasping increasingly beautiful aspects of living and abstaining from wasting time on getting a charge out of pleasures don't enhance personal satisfaction.

Make an investment account.
Monetary opportunity is a piece of minimalism. Having a bank account and frequently sending money to the record urges you to proceed notwithstanding carrying on with a progressively minimalist lifestyle because it will guarantee you cut out needless memberships and costs. Additionally, it will make you all the more financially steady.

Dress with less.
Having few shoes, garments and extras may sound extraordinary but it is a decent method to start carrying on with a minimalist lifestyle. It makes life less intricate and decreases clutter in your closet.

Appreciate the voyage of carrying on with a minimalist lifestyle.
Finally, when you've embraced or chosen to carry on with a minimalist lifestyle, welcome the seemingly insignificant details you have and in every case live each and every day expressing gratitude toward yourself for the way you've taken.

Quit multitasking.
There is no such thing as multitasking. It is a legend, a fantasy. Numerous individuals have faith in it and pride themselves of being astounding multitaskers. But all they do is to trick themselves. Firmly having faith in something does not really make it genuine. Scientific research has indicated on many occasions that the human cerebrum isn't fit for

multitasking. All you do is to change starting with one movement then onto the next, which can drastically decrease your efficiency. Try not to clutter your work process and life by seeking after different exercises all the while. Rather, center around doing just a single thing at any given moment. Do whatever you do with the best consideration and consideration. Dispose of diversions and endeavor to conquer the compulsion to multitask. "Singletasking" will assist you with being increasingly gainful in what you do. It increases your focus and will dramatically affect the yield of your work. Minimalism is tied in with concentrating on what's really critical – with more prominent consideration.

Assess your objectives and desire.
We as a whole have objectives. They influence us to get up every morning to proceed with the quest for our fantasies. Our objectives and desire significantly shape the lives we are living. But not all objectives are advantageous. Not all desire are good with a minimalistic lifestyle. It is therefore essential to assess if your objectives are still in accordance with the needs you set in stage 1 of this list. Question if the quest for your objectives will increase the value of your life. Set aside yourself opportunity to ponder the result of your objectives. Is it the result deserving of your time and exertion? In the meantime, it's critical to lessen the measure of objectives you seek after. Try not to clutter your life with a wide assortment of objectives that you seek after just pitifully. Concentrate on setting yourself a predetermined number of objectives and seek after these with your most prominent consideration and tirelessness. You could even venture to such an extreme as to minimalize to just a single objective. It will push you to enormously diminish pressure and to focus on the objective with the most noteworthy need.

Begin small.
When it comes to simplifying your life, it's critical to keep up a slow dimension of progress. If you set yourself the yearning objective to de-clutter your whole house or level inside about fourteen days, you may overpower yourself.

Rather, begin small and work yourself gradually towards an increasingly shortsighted presence. Rather than cleansing a whole room, center around smaller areas of the room. Complete one region at once until the point that the whole room is not so much cluttered but rather more minimalistic. For example, center around de-cluttering one segment of your rack after another.

Live purposely.
Another imperative aspect of turning into a minimalist is to live right now and to live more intentionally. To do this current, it's imperative to shift your consideration from the past or future to this exact second. Do whatever it takes not to point the finger at yourself for what occurred in the past and attempt to quit agonizing over what's to come. When you live in the past or the future, you deny the present snapshot of its delight and power. Understand that you can neither make things that occurred in the past fixed nor would you be able to impact what occurs later on. Rather, use the present to construct the fundament for a more promising time to come. Correspondingly, use the experiences/botches you've made in the past as imperative exercises. Living all the more intentionally will assist you with spending your time in a progressively significant and important way. Simplify your life and investigate the satisfaction living at the time has to offer.

Limit screen time and media utilization.
The time we spend on mechanical devices adds pointless commotion to our lives. Also, the negligent utilization of media includes more intricacy than it simplifies. If you spend a lot of your tedious different types of media (TV, films, Internet, papers, and so forth.) at that point these things will significantly shape the manner in which you think and feel. The additional time you go through with media, the more impact it will apply over your life. If media utilization commands your life, your contemplations and activities will be ruled by it as well. It can extraordinarily influence your convictions and your general point of view. The huge issue,

be that as it may, is to completely grasp the impact of media at the forefront of your thoughts. This is especially difficult if your reasoning is still extraordinarily impacted by media. There's solitary one approach to find the negative effect of all these things on your life, which is by subsequently disposing of them from your life. It's moderately easy to disregard the above as hogwash if you're still intensely impacted by media. But you will be astounded of the significant difference disengaging and turning things off can make.

Ask yourself

Does this assistance to live more minimalistic? You can incredibly contribute to the minimization of your life by settling on choices that are more in accordance with a minimalistic lifestyle. If you can do this, your purchasing propensities will incredibly change. This thusly will assist you with avoiding de-cluttering your life in any case. So whenever you will meet a choice, ask yourself if it will help you minimalize or if it just includes pointless clamor. Offer yourself the conversation starter if the choice you will meet will simplify your life or not. If it doesn't contribute to a minimalist lifestyle, rethink if it is the best alternative for you.

MINIMALISM AND DECLUTTERING

SIMPLE WAYS TO

SAVE MONEY

Set a reserve funds objective

Use our Savings calculatorto perceive how your reserve funds will develop.

A few people think that its difficult to get persuaded about sparing, but it's frequently a lot easier if you set an objective.

Your initial step is to have some crisis reserve funds – money to fall back on if you have a crisis, for example, an evaporator breakdown or if you can't work for some time.

Attempt to get three months of costs in an easy or moment get to account.

Try not to stress if you can't spare this straight away, but keep it as an objective to go for.

The most ideal approach to set aside extra money is to pay some money into a bank account each month.

When you've put aside your secret stash, conceivable funds objectives to consider may include:

> › Buying a vehicle without applying for a new line of credit
> › Taking an occasion without stressing over the bills when you get back
> › Having some additional money to draw on while you're on maternity or paternity leave

Record your costs

The initial step to setting aside some money is to make sense of the amount you spend. Monitor all your costs—that implies each espresso, household thing and money tip. When you have your information, arrange the numbers by classifications, for example, gas, basic supplies and home loan, and aggregate each sum. Consider utilizing your Mastercard or bank proclamations to assist you with this. Bank of America customers can use the Spending and Budgeting tool, which automatically sorts your exchanges for easier planning in the portable application or on the web.

Instructions to set up a financial plan

Do you have more than one record? New administrations mean you would now be able to see all your records in a solitary keeping money application.

The initial step to taking control of your funds is completing a financial plan.

It will require a little exertion, but it's an extraordinary method to get a brisk preview of the money you have coming in and going out.

Setting up a spending implies you're:

> › Less likely to finish up in debt
> › Less likely to get captured out by sudden expenses
> › More likely to have a decent FICO assessment
> › More likely to be acknowledged for a home loan or advance
> › Able to spot areas where you can make reserve funds
> › In an incredible position to set something aside for a vacation, another vehicle, or another treat

Plan on setting aside somemoney

Since you've influenced a financial plan, to make an investment funds classification inside it. Endeavor to spare 10 to 15 percent of your pay. If your costs are high to the point that you can't spare that much, it may be an ideal opportunity to curtail. To do as such, identify superfluous items that you can spend less on, for example, amusement and feasting out, and discover approaches to save money on your settled month to month costs.

Tip: Consider the money you put into investment funds a customary cost, like staple goods, to strengthen great reserve funds propensities.

Pick something to put something aside for
Extraordinary compared to other approaches to set aside some money is to set an objective. Begin by considering what you should want to put something aside for—maybe you're getting hitched, arranging an excursion or putting something aside for retirement. At that point make sense of how much money you'll need and to what extent it may take you to spare it. If you have a Bank of America account, you can use the Picture My Goals tool to set up and keep tabs on your development toward your objectives in the portable application.

Here are a few instances of short-and long haul objectives:

Present moment (1– 3 years)

Emergency finance (3– 9 months of everyday costs, to be safe)
Vacation
Down installment for a vehicle
Long haul (4+ years)

Down installment on a home or a rebuilding venture
Your tyke's instruction
Retirement

If you're putting something aside for retirement or your tyke's instruction, consider putting that money into a venture record, for example, an IRA or 529 arrangement. While ventures accompany hazards and can lose money, they also make the open door for exacerbated returns if you plan for an occasion far ahead of time. See step No. 6 for more subtleties.

Take Control of Your Bank Fees
As was the case with your Mastercards, you are most likely also being charged pointless or overinflated bank

expenses. ATM expenses, exchange charges, month to month account keeping expenses, and so on. In disengagement, these charges probably won't appear much, but they do all include.

The bank expenses you are paying might just be debatable or at any rate sufficiently adaptable for you to roll out a few improvements.

Stop for a moment to talk with your ledger supervisor and examine how you can potentially rebuild your financial balances and your pulling back propensities to enable you to spare money. They will gladly enable you to out and will furnish you with proposals on how you can lessen these expenses. And obviously, if you're not fulfilled, at that point search around and locate a superior arrangement.

Take Control of Personal Taxes
The vast majority of us set aside charge time for conceded. We pay what we are intended to pay and we only every once in a long while question regardless of whether we could have saved money.

Stop for a moment to talk with an expense bookkeeper and clarify your circumstance. Educate them that you might want to talk about ideas for making good on less regulatory obligation. Ask them for proposals and direction about what you could use as a duty derivation, and/or how you could potentially spend or put your money so as to decrease the measure of assessment you pay toward the finish of the budgetary year.

Being savvier in the manner in which you handle your charges could potentially spare you thousands of dollars for every year.

Settle on your needs
After your costs and pay, your objectives are likely to have the greatest effect on how you allocate your reserve funds. Make sure to recall long haul objectives—it's essential that making arrangements for retirement doesn't take a

secondary lounge to shorter-term needs. Figure out how to organize your funds objectives so you have a reasonable thought of where to begin sparing. For instance, if you realize you will need to supplant your vehicle sooner rather than later, you could begin putting money away for one at this point.

Getting a good deal on Your Car Expenses
Statistically, in the western world, the vast lion's share of individuals possess a vehicle. It could be a vehicle or even potentially a bike or motorbike. Regardless of what sort of vehicle it will be, it's in all probability going to be one of your greatest continuous costs. As it were, it continually empties money from your pocket every week with continuous fuel, upkeep, and protection costs.

It could be contended that a vehicle is an extravagance. It's unquestionably something that many could manage without, but the bother this would cause could potentially risk an individual's salary, for example their capacity to get the chance to work every day. Be that as it may, there are approaches to set aside some money without setting off to the limits and moving your vehicle. How about we investigate these ideas underneath.

Vehicle Maintenance is Paramount
An unmaintained vehicle is just a waste receptacle for money. Adjusting your vehicle routinely will in all likelihood be undeniably more savvy over the long haul than paying for administration and parts when things separate. It's also more secure to drive and conceivably will enable you to dodge unforeseen medicinal costs that emerge from vehicle mishaps that outcome from breakdowns.

Vehicle upkeep also encompasses seemingly insignificant details, for example, ensuring you are driving with the ideal tire weight. When your tires are too level there is more drag and contact with the street, which makes the vehicle's motor work harder, which in this manner consumes more fuel and tosses money down the deplete.

Get a good deal on Insurance

Keeping up your vehicle is clearly critical, but so is protection. Indeed, there are numerous individuals who drive around with no protection inclusion. And truly, they positively set aside some money temporarily. Without any mishaps, they don't have anything to stress over. Be that as it may, what are the assurances?

Vehicle protection gives you genuine feelings of serenity just in case you are engaged with a mishap. Indeed, it will remove money from your pocket that you could have rather used to satisfy your charge cards, or saved into your rainy day account or investment account. In any case, recall that when you're engaged with a mishap "where no doubt about it", you're not just paying for the fix of your own vehicle, but also for the fix of the other vehicle you beat up.

It is, obviously, essential to look for the best protection bargain. Likewise, you can also consult with your present supplier at a superior cost. Potentially you right now have an "Under 25 Driver" alternative for you that adds 20 dollars to your approach every month. Potentially that is something you could manage without. Along these lines, you could potentially spare yourself a couple of hundred dollars for each year. In any case, be mindful so as not to lessen your choices to such a dimension, to the point that you're scarcely canvassed in case of a mishap.

Stay away from These Money Wasting Driving Tendencies

Owning a vehicle is fantastic. It takes you from A to B, in any case, the fuel can also cost you dearly. Nonetheless, there are a few straightforward things you can do that will help make your vehicle unquestionably increasingly prudent and productive.

For example, did you realize that utilizing cooling can diminish the eco-friendliness of your vehicle by up to 10 percent? This is especially valid at lower speeds. It, therefore, bodes well to open a window while driving gradually in suburbia. In any case, at higher rates, the open window can make drag which also brings down the eco-friendliness of your vehicle. In such cases, at higher velocities (on roads) it bodes well to siphon up the cooling instead of opening a window.

You will also consume fuel faster if you drive erratically. By flighty, I mean braking frequently, quickening rapidly, and weaving forcefully all through traffic paths. Pick rather to back off and relentless your driving. This will assist you with saving fuel costs over the long haul.

Set aside extra money by Being a More Savvy Driver
Here are some further proposals to enable you to save money on fuel costs:

> › Avoid driving amid surge hour traffic.
> › Use voyage control to smooth out your driving.
> › Remove extreme load from your vehicle, especially from the storage compartment.
> › Minimize sitting time at traffic lights.
> › Consolidate all your errands into one trek.

These are all exceptionally basic and clear ideas. So direct in certainty that it may appear as however these progressions won't make a big deal about a difference, anyway as time goes on you will put more money ideal over into your pocket.

Picking Alternate Transportation Options
Owning a vehicle is costly. Not exclusively are there support costs, protection charges, fuel costs, but there are also enlistment expenses. If you are not kidding about setting aside some money, then you could abandon your vehicle for the present and drive by riding your bicycle or utilizing open transport.

On the other hand, if you like to clutch your vehicle, then you could consider carpooling with a work pal. That way you will potentially slice your fuel costs down the middle through the span of a year.

Pick the correct tools

If you're putting something aside for momentary objectives, consider utilizing these FDIC-guaranteed store accounts:

> › Savings account
> › Certificate of store (CD), which secures your money for a settled timeframe at a rate that is typically higher than investment accounts

For long haul objectives consider

> › FDIC-protected individual retirement accounts (IRAs), which are impose productive bank accounts
> › Securities, for example, stocks or common assets. These venture items are accessible through speculation accounts with a merchant. Keep in mind that securities are not protected by the FDIC, are not stores or different commitments of a bank and are not ensured by a bank. They are liable to venture dangers, including the conceivable loss of your vital.

You don't need to pick only one record. Take a gander at all of your choices and consider things like equalization essentials, expenses and loan costs so you can pick the blend that will enable you to best put something aside for your objectives.

Make sparing programmed

All banks offer computerized exchanges between your checking and investment accounts. You can pick when, how much and where to exchange money or even split your immediate store so a part of each paycheck goes specifically into your bank account. Part your immediate store and setting up mechanized exchanges are straightforward approaches to set aside extra money since you don't need to consider it, and it generally lessens the compulsion to spend the money.

Watch your funds develop

Survey your financial plan and check your advancement consistently. Not exclusively will this assistance you adhere to your own reserve funds plan, but it also causes you identify and settle issues rapidly. These straightforward approaches to spare may even move you to spare more money each day and hit your objectives faster.

Setting aside extra money Around the Home
There are a lot of basic things we can do around the home that can assist us with starting setting aside extramoney. Inside this area we should investigate three noteworthy home-related costs and the small changes we can start making that will keep more money in our pockets.

Save money on Your Water Expenses
We use water each day. We clean up, wash stuff, do the dishes, water the garden, use the latrine, cook, and we even beverage this stuff. Given this, water is a major piece of our lives and — except if you're living in the nation — tragically, it's not something we get for nothing from earth.

Figuring out how to deal with the water you use all the more successfully can assist you with saving a lot of moneythrough the span of a year. Consider for example the accompanying water sparing ideas:

> › Wash your garments less regularly.
> › Reduce the measure of yard watering days.
> › Install a keen sprinkler framework.
> › Take shorter showers and challenge yourselfto use a clock.
> › Avoid cleaning up that typically expend a lot of water.
> › Half flush the can rather than the normal full flush.
> › Turn off water taps when not being used, for example, while brushing your teeth.

By making these strides you could potentially divide your water utilization costs and therefore potentially spare yourself many dollars every year.

Save money on Your Electricity Expenses

The other significant but vital cost comes as power. In any case, there are a few things you can do to cut your expenses here as well. Here are a few ideas:

> › Invest in sufficient protection to keep your home cool During summer and warm During winter. Less warming and cooling required.
> › Don't set your warming too high, and your cooling too low. Also, make sure to close your windows.
> › Install durable energy-sparing lights around the home.
> › Turn off superfluous lights or diminish them to spare power.
> › Unplug gadgets and machines that are not being used.
> › Use washing machines and dryers During off-crest times. This is for the individuals who are on-crest and off-top power designs.

Moreover, you could, obviously, arrange a superior manage your capacity supplier. If they won't give you a superior arrangement, at that point basically take your business somewhere else.

By making these strides you could potentially spare yourself several dollars for every year on power costs.

Save money on Your Rental Expenses

The third significant cost comes as rental expenses. Leasing a home, level or condo is a transaction. You get what you're ready to arrange. The better arrangement you can arrange the less money you will spend on your living facilities.

You can anyway also spare a lot of lease by livingwith other individuals. Offering your rental costs to others can be a standout amongst the most significant cost-sparing choices you will ever make.

DIFFERENT LEVELS OF MINIMALISM

Minimalism of Desire

This is when you anticipate less from the world. You acknowledge what you have and given things a chance to unfurl without a feeling of privilege. It doesn't mean you quit wanting a superior life. It just methods you let go of the harshness you feel when things don't go your direction.

Minimalism of Possessions

This is when you claim just what you need. You dispose of things that don't serves you and don't purchase things only for owning them. This reaches out to the money you procure. You make the most of it and spend it just on things that will fulfill you and your friends and family and sound. This also implies you don't chase unreasonable measures of money that you don't really need or couldn't in any way, shape or form spend.

Minimalism of Relations

This one's difficult to clarify, coz I don't want you to misunderstand the thought. When you practice minimalism in your relations, you don't gather individuals like social identifications. You quit checking what number of companions you have. On Facebook as well as, in actuality. Because you understand that the measure of people you know doesn't make a difference so much as the nature of the relationship you share with those people. So you keep in your life just the individuals who advance it with their adoration, the individuals who fulfill you and bolster you with all their heart. It's difficult to rehearse this kind of minimalism however, coz if you're not watchful you may turn into a relationship Nazi, who makes a decision about individuals on the value of what they can improve the situation you. This dimension isn't tied in with dismissing all but a select number of individuals. It's tied in with seeing those you invest your energy with for who they genuinely are and ensuring you possess enough energy for the individuals who mean the most to you.

Minimalism of sound
When you practice this sort of minimalism you endeavor to make as little clamor as conceivable. It's about just utilizing the sounds you completely need to. In this way, if you can say something smoothly and unobtrusively, there's no need to shout. If you can move smoothly and gradually, why surge and make a frenzy? This reaches out to minimalism of words, which basically implies you state just what you should to express what is on your mind.

Minimalism of thought
In which you practice care, to lessen over the top reasoning, settle on basic leadership progressively productive and take out pressure and nervousness.

Interest
Those who fall into the curiosity stage may have quite recently found minimalism and the advantages of living with less. At this stage, you're fascinated with the thought and you may end up spending incalculable hours perusing each blog, book, and Facebook page you can discover.

Readiness
At this stage you have discovered you're prepared to roll out the improvement and are presently mentally setting yourself up. You may have started arranging your assets in to heaps and wind up developing increasingly more OK with dividing your things.

Cleansing
Those who fall into the PURGING stage are prepared to start, and may have even felt a jazzed opportunity from hurling their first trash pack loaded up with things. Amid this

stage you'll wind up hurling boxes, sacks, and perhaps dumpsters loaded up with things you never again need or have been clutching to be safe. We will in general remain in this phase for some time, and may even come back to it again later on.

Organize

After you've cleansed you start to sort out what remains. During this stage it's tied in with discovering balance in your home and arranging things such that will fill your heart with joy to day life easier.

Avoidance

This stage may happen whenever or after any of the above stages. During this stage we end up becoming exhausted, tired, or baffled with our new lifestyles and we may start to dodge any more advancement. It's critical when you achieve this phase to push through it and spotlight on the positives.

Maintain

After we have cleansed and composed we'll achieve the upkeep organize. Right now we've set up our accepted procedures and it turns out to be second nature to declutter and sort out. Amid this stage you may wind up doing small episodes of cleansing and re-sorting out your space – and that is flawlessly ordinary!

Growth

Your voyage through minimalism will be an extensive one, but it will at last help you to develop. In this stage we've accomplished some type of development and maybe intelligence through our voyage. We can use this opportunity to spread our insight to other people.

ALEXANDRA JESSEN

WHAT IS THE DOWNSIDE OF MINIMALISM?

People may believe you're unusual at first. It requires investment to teach your loved ones concerning for what reason you're doing things along these lines, and it takes a little mettle to be different. It's totally justified, despite all the trouble. Leo Babauta of mnmlist.com

There are sure malicious aspects at the edge of any essential development, and minimalism is the same. If you fixate on tallying your things or about disposing of all of your stuff or about carrying on with an extraordinary traveling lifestyle, at that point you're overlooking the main issue of minimalism inside and out. Not that it's inappropriate to check your stuff or to venture to the far corners of the planet, it's simply that minimalism isn't about that stuff, it's not tied in with tallying or "deserting everything," and it's absolutely not about fixation. Minimalism is just a tool to get of life's abundance so you can concentrate on life's critical things, things like relations and seeking after your passions and self-improvement and contributing to others genuinely. Joshua from The Minimalists

As far as I can see, no, there isn't, but I am really new to this! Perhaps the unavoidable actuality a few people don't understand this way and the related decisions, but this isn't so sad. Laura of minimoblog.it

I figure individuals can get too made up for lost time in tallying quantities of things, paring down underneath what's their solace point, and they lose site of why they began the minimalist adventure in any case. Equalization is vital! Robyn Devine of Minimalist Knitter

MINIMALISM AND DECLUTTERING

There are scarcely any drawbacks to minimalism, but at times it's difficult to disclose it to people who have shut personalities. In some cases individuals simply would prefer not to understand minimalism, they see what we're doing and they simply want to contend or expel it as a trend. The greater part of those people are exceptionally joined to their things, and they are hesitant to quit expending because they associate a specific importance with their utilization, they are too appended to a belief system that their stuff brings them satisfaction. Fortunately, after some time, minimalism uncovers all of its favorable circumstances all alone. So if you're tolerant with those people, their brains will open, and they will understand eventually. Ryan from The Minimalists

It's an extremely self-uncovering procedure and lifestyle. When we start to expel the diversion and clutter from our life, our brains are obvious to dive further into our very own essence. It tends to be difficult at first as we are compelled to think about our intentions in gathering all this stuff in any case, but it is a decent procedure to great through. It improves us individuals at last. Joshua Becker of Becoming Minimalist

It has been challenging to converse with family and companions about our decision to possess less things. Regularly individuals feel that our different lifestyle decision is an immediate remark without anyone else. To keep discussions light, I generally state this works for us but it's not for everybody. In all actuality I feel that some level of minimalism, scaling back and dismissing commercialization is gainful for everybody. Rachel Jonat of Minimalist Mom

What I've discovered difficult is that numerous individuals respond emphatically — "Minimalism sounds extraordinary! I ought to do that." — but then they remain stuck in stuff. There's a touch of weight, advocating a cause you realize will enhance individuals' lives, if just they would simply participate. Obviously, this is an expectation filled drawback. Anybody can begin whenever. And people do! That is one inspiration that keeps me offering a life of straightforward living to other people. Dave Bruno from A Guy Named Dave

None! I genuinely can't consider anything. Meg Wolfe of Minimalist Woman

I think the most essential thing to recall is... our identity could really compare to what we call ourselves. Minimalists and hoarders alike, let the emphasis be on how you treat people, and carry on with your life, rather than how much stuff you have or don't have.

MINIMALISM AND DECLUTTERING

THE MISTAKES OF MINIMALISM

Minimalism is winding up increasingly more prevalent for an assortment of reasons, especially with the "style de jour" being "easy costly"(as my supervisor has named it), which has some extremely solid minimalism veins going through it and the use of a couple of great created things versus, a rack brimming with shabby clutter. Who knows why the minimalist pattern is blasting – It may be because many individuals feel that lifeoutsidethe house is getting SO riotous that a progressively minimalist structure for the insides will encourage counter that, or perhaps because with the consistently expanding costs on pretty much everything in the stores we think it is presently alright to purchase $400 material cover that is the same as a vintage form that costs an eighth of the cost. Others may lean progressively minimalist essentially because they want to dispose of the stuff they don't need or use – which may also be at fault on the book that I read alongside pretty much every other person "The Life Changing Magic of Tidying Up". Whatever it is, minimalism is slanting.

But minimalism isn't exactly as easy to accomplish as individuals may think. TBH, as somebody who completes a ton of prop styling for their activity "toning it down would be best" in my case, and getting that "simply enough stuff" easy negligible look is quite hard. As a plan strategy, minimalism has been confounded and misused by numerous individuals, as far as I have seen on the web and through a few pictures that are springing up, so we will have a brisk take a gander at the basic errors that people make when they attempt to transform their homes into a minimalist heaven. That is to say, if you will upgrade the look of your home and hurl it all away to kick off said new lifestyle, then you should do it appropriately!

Put Off Starting Because You Don't Like The "Tenets"

One thing that kept me away from beginning with minimalism was my false conviction that it was an "all or nothing" lifestyle. I'd perused a huge amount of blog entries and articles about people who just possessed 100 things or who lived in modest houses and I was fascinated by their lifestyles, but I realized it wasn't for me.

I realized I was continually going to keep some wistful things (old letters, and so forth.) and I liked having a couple of knickknacks. I would not like to live in an all white house and I was never going to get by with only one sets of shoes! I liked living with less but I realized I was never going to be like the general population I read about on the web.

I didn't think minimalism was appropriate for me until the point that I understood ... there's solitary one guideline with minimalism.

Minimalism is tied in with living with goal and being aware of what you allow in your life (things, ideas, individuals, and so forth.).

That is it; there are no other "rules". Minimalism is close to home and what it looks like in your life is dependent upon you. As you long as you're being straightforward with yourself about what adds value or conveys bliss to your life, at that point you're a minimalist. Your adaptation of minimalism probably won't resemble my rendition of minimalism—and that is alright. All things considered, minimalism is a tool to enable you to carry on with a life you adore—not a true objective.

Try Not To Lose Yourself

The web is a unimaginable place to get roused. I personally can say my whole lifestyle has drastically changed, and to improve things, from being propelled by others on the web. I have gone veggie lover, drastically diminished my waste, decluttered the majority of my stuff and set out on a voyage of self value since seeing others do likewise. In any case, I have committed the error en route of losing myself and my uniqueness. It very well may be easy to simply duplicate what another person is doing and seek it works after you too, but this shockingly doesn't usually work out. We're all totally different, have different existences, have different expectations, wants and needs. We therefore need to each use minimalism (or any lifestyle so far as that is concerned) in different ways. Your adaptation of minimalism will be totally different to mine. Keep in mind that minimalism isn't a challenge. The essentials of minimalism are to relinquish craving and owning stuff to decide your value, and yet when we begin to use minimalism, it very well may entice decide our value based off how little we claim. Try not to allow this to occur, keep your limits and don't lose your identity in the quest for this lifestyle.

Relax

I'm the kind of individual who settles on a choice, clicks my fingers and wants things done straight away. I will in general go for things full power, which can have its advantages and drawbacks. While I had the inspiration to get things sorted out, it wound up disappointing when the truth it wouldn't occur immediately began to rise. I understood I needed to take things easy. I wasn't going to declutter my whole life medium-term. I wouldn't turn a disorganized closet that I had been gathering for the last decade into an insignificant case closet by one week from now. But after some time I understood how mind blowing this time was. I adapted beyond what I would ever have envisioned a straightforward decluttering of my stuff would educate me. During this long procedure of decluttering I was ready to reflect, search inside, understand where I had been, and where I wanted to go. So my recommendation is make things stride by venture such that bodes well for you. Offer yourself a reprieve and relax. Begin with an aspects of your life that is in especially over-burden (for me this was my closet) and go from that point.

Try Not To Make It Unattainable

What is minimalism about? It is to lessen and to just. Minimalism isn't quantified by how little you possess or how white your stylish is. Try not to let it to end up another perfect that you've been sold that you can't satisfy. It needs to stay feasible and comprehensive, as opposed to unattainable and restrictive. Set yourself feasible objectives, for example, clearing all the surfaces in your home, or disposing of a container of things you don't need any longer. There doesn't need to be any limits. Limits just make things farfetched and harder to accomplish. So the main objectives you ought to set for yourself are ones that are inside reach.

Try not to Buy New Stuff

When I originally began decluttering, I gave myself a shopping boycott. Especially when it came to garments. I understood I had all that I needed, and the impulse to purchase new things needed to be killed. It was a tremendous expectation to learn and adapt for me as for a very long time I generally had a considerable rundown of things I wanted in my closet, my cosmetics sack or whatever. I realized that I needed to relinquish this steady longing for new things and spotlight on sorting out and getting free. The best part is, this procedure did what I trusted it would do and quite a lot more. I never again long to go out on the town to shop, I am more chivalrous than any other time in recent memory when I do need to go out on the town to shop for something, I have turned out to be quite a lot more thankful for all the things I have in my life, and I have spared such a great amount of money simultaneously. So one of the greatest things you can do when you first begin is to instruct yourself to state no to new things. Concentrate on decluttering, limiting and getting free, and discover fulfillment in that (but also don't pummel yourself if you do slip and unintentionally purchase something new, simply proceed onward and gain from it).

Try Not To Put Pressure On Yourself

Don't put weight on yourself. This procedure shouldn't finish up being a distressing one. If you go out and purchase something and think twice about it a short time later, don't thump yourself, simply gain from it! Consider how it affected you and how perhaps you could improve the situation next time. Slip-ups are there to be gained from and if we didn't make them we wouldn't get much of anywhere in our life. Keep in mind that is anything but a goal, but an adventure. Regardless i'm learning regular, committing errors, coming up short and getting back up once more. It is the thing that makes us human, improves us develop and move toward becoming individuals progressing in the direction of our objectives. Relinquish the weight and appreciate the experience!

No Personality

Insignificant DOES NOT EQUAL an absence of identity, but frequently an exposed room is regularly one without simply that. This is a typical mistake in minimalist homes, but running minimalist with your plan doesn't imply that you need to dispose of the sentiment of human nearness and identity in your home. Definitely, keep things straightforward and refined but give yourself some significant craftsmanship, a plant or greenery, a few books that work with your design, and a couple of beautiful (but utilitarian) embellishments.

Doing Without Functionality For Style

Minimalism is, to some degree, about having what you need and nothing more. A few people tragically take this excessively literally. I have done this without anyone else's help, thinking in my mind "this seat is so basic, so refined and so sleek" when in actuality it ought to state "this seat is sufficiently agreeable to sit on it for .0234 seconds previously you want to move to a different seat". So when choosing your furnishings, stockpiling, or embellishment decisions remember this. Because despite the fact that it might appear to be chic to have a smooth home office that is finished with a reasonable work area, a couple of small adornments and a light, that is REALLY just not handy. You need a considerable amount more as this article appears. Along these lines, if you've stripped things to such a degree, to the point that usefulness has been sacrificed, at that point you've gone too far!

Capacity
Because you are a recently discovered individual from the minimalist mafia doesn't imply that you don't need cautiously thought about capacity. Regardless of who you think you are, or what style or stylistic theme you use, each individual on earth will need a smidgen of capacity, so get yourself a piece that will work for what you need (regardless of whether it is vacant for the principal tad).

Clear Walls
I secured this one a couple of days prior and it does fairly fall under the "No Personality" segment, but it needs calling out once more. I am all for minimalism, but regardless of how refined and insignificant you are, exposed and clear walls will make your space feel chilly, unfilled and generic. Along these lines, in spite of the fact that you probably won't be into a massive gallery wall, think of some as exceptionally very much arranged craftsmanship that works inside your space to bring some life and shading up on those walls of yours.

Shading
I realize you may feel that I supreme HATE shading, but that isn't the case. Indeed, I do veer more towards the tonal and textural sides of things versus implanting things with brilliant hues but it doesn't imply that I loathe it. Especially on account of minimalism, when things may be exceptionally simplified, the case for shading turns out to be significantly increasingly imperative. If you will keep it basic consider injecting some refined shading in to keep the enthusiasm for the room alive.

MINIMALISM AND DECLUTTERING

Terrible Furniture Layout

Many individuals assume that you can't really turn out badly with the format of the furnishings in a minimalist home. All things considered, what amount of furniture can you really have when you take this plan course of "toning it down would be best"? The issue is that the design of your furnishings can in any case appear to be disordered and swarmed; regardless of whether you have not very many things in there and there's a nice measure of room to lay it all out in. Along these lines, when you start to go negligible still remember the customary guidelines of styling and furniture position and don't trade your couch for a thin lined seat and then two straightforward side seats that may finish of doing the opposite you had proposed for the room.

So whether you are into it or not, simply recollect that negligible doesn't amount to nothing, and basic doesn't mean without identity. Obviously make your home work for you and for each standard there is a reason to break it. Simply don't go out resembling a distinct, tragic space bereft of well... anything. To enable you to begin here are a couple of my most loved insignificant yet beautiful and useful things.

Dispose of The Duplicates

As a Beginner Minimalist bear in mind to dispose of copies. You can alter down somewhat more without agony. Check for things that fill a similar need in your life and alter all but one of them.

What number of sets of boots do you need? Do you need 5 winter coats? What number of angling bars do you need? What number of handbags do you need?

Check the kitchen and carport for copy things to alter down. If you are anything like me, you are a sucker for tools and contraptions. Scale back, lessen, reuse, reuse and reestablish.

This will add to streamlining your life and help you maintain a strategic distance from choice weakness. It can even go far to soothing worry from your life relying upon what number of copy things you claim.

Unfriend and Unfollow The Peanut Gallery
Try not to falter to unfriend and unfollow your minimalist spoilers mentally and now and then physically. We as a whole have counterfeit individuals on our companion's rundown who's continually posting hostile jokes and inadequately explored data. Try not to give false companions a chance to obstruct your advancement. Unfriend them for some time.

Great loved ones can be brutal when they don't understand something. Under the appearance of thinking about you, loved ones can be merciless with analysis, threatening vibe and over association trying to change your conduct to their preferring.

You can't simply unfriend and unfollow great loved ones. They assume a critical job in your life and will dependably be near.

You can unfriend and unfollow them symbolically. Stand solid against this kind of negative conduct should it emerge. Try not to contend and argue your case. Simply grin and proceed with your advancement towards understanding the minimalist lifestyle. When you unfriend and unfollow them symbolically they will take note.

They will also see you are increasingly glad, progressively sorted out, less focused, have progressively extra money and time to make incredible recollections with them. This may stand out enough to be noticed and you may then actually have a savvy discussion about the advantages of carrying on with the minimalist lifestyle.

Making A Decision About Other People
When you finally come to the heart of the matter where you "get" minimalism—you've scaled back your stuff and you've begun to contemplate your life—it's easy to begin making a decision about individuals who aren't minimalists.

MINIMALISM AND DECLUTTERING

(Some of the time this isn't deliberate; you're simply amped up for how your life has changed and you can't understand why everybody is ready!)

In any case, purposeful or not, being judgmental is unkind and useless.

I understand your enthusiasm about minimalism, but the most ideal approach to get the message out is to be a positive good example with your own life. Discussion about how minimalism has transformed you and answer questions if they're asked, but don't remark contrarily on other individuals' lives (either to their face or away from plain view). Life is an adventure; we have different ways and we're all at different stages.

Energize, but don't lecture. Move, but don't pass judgment.

Starting Minimalist Keeping Things Just In Case
Keeping Things Just In Case, for what? If you are not utilizing it to dispose of or give it away. Anything that does not increase the value of your life or fulfill you ought to be reexamined.

If it doesn't summon a positive emotion or if you would not promptly supplant it if lost it likely ought to be sold, given or disposed of.

Trust your intuition and not your emotions. If there was a case for the thing it would have happened as of now. In the remote possibility that you disposed of and the thing you currently need, simply use something you officially claim or obtain the thing from another hotspot for that one time use.

As a starting minimalist, you ought to rapidly learn not to emotionally clutch things in the event that something goes wrong. Release those things and release the worry of owning, putting away and overseeing them as well.

ALEXANDRA JESSEN

CORE PRINCIPLES TO MAXIMIZE LIVING AND LIVE ON PURPOSE

Feeling that what you're doing has a genuine reason and implying that issues to you can have a colossal effect in your life. It makes getting up every day the most energizing thing on the planet. You can hardly wait to begin. Disregard endeavoring to constrain yourself to buckle down, it turns out to be increasingly critical to remind yourself to take breaks to eat!

But how might we develop a progressively important life? The appropriate response is usually confounded. It can rely upon numerous components. I've recorded 10 ideas that I accept will enable you to discover significance in your life consistently, with the goal that you can hardly wait to get up toward the beginning of the day and see what the day will bring.

For what reason do I need to know my qualities?
Qualities give us our feeling of direction. On an authority level, when we line up with our qualities once a day, we have more energy and feel progressively satisfied because we are driving from what's vital to us. When we don't line up with our qualities, we feel less credible and progress toward becoming demotivated about our day by day lives, which reflects in our initiative.

Consider it a tree: values are our foundations that keep us grounded in what's vital to us. The quality of the qualities decides the quality of the storage compartment, branches, leaves and natural product from year to year. A solid tree bolsters the biological community around it; a pioneer with solid qualities underpins the authoritative culture.

MINIMALISM AND DECLUTTERING

How Do I Find My Values?

Qualities are like a compass that guides us toward our "actual north." Let's survey an incredible exercise to help you unmistakably identify your fundamental beliefs. Would you be able to recall a minute where your life couldn't beat that? When everything felt adjusted? It might have even felt like the greatest day of your life. Set aside some opportunity to recall this pinnacle minute and pursue these means:

Portray this pinnacle minute in detail.

If you are chipping away at this activity alone, compose the depiction. If you are doing this activity with somebody, talk about this minute for 2-3 minutes while the other individual takes notes.

Consider and examine what esteems are conspicuous in this specific pinnacle minute.

From the pinnacle minute portrayed above, you could state I esteem:

Being outside

Working with people to build up their potential

Being daring

Pick the esteem or qualities that you've identified as most essential to you.

(Keep in mind that your qualities apply to both your own and expert universes.)

From the three potential qualities I identified above, I pick 'audacious' as the one that is most vital to me in both my vocation and individual life.

Characterize what the picked esteem or qualities intend to YOU.

To me, 'courageous' signifies picking an unusual way, attempting heaps of new things, going to new places (literally and metaphorically), investigating choices and tinkering with ideas to discover arrangements.

Proceed with the procedure until the point that you characterize around 5 fundamental beliefs.

How Do I Put My Values in real life?

Presently it's a great opportunity to incorporate your qualities. Here are three handy tips to enable you to start the procedure.

Seek after Your Passion

I trust everybody should seek after their passion in life. It's what makes life worth living, and gives our lives genuine significance and reason. Each time you take a shot at something you cherish, it makes delight inside you don't like anything else. Figuring out how to use your passions to offer back to the world will give your life extreme significance.

If you can't oversee (or aren't prepared) to chip away at your passion professionally, make certain and set aside a few minutes for it consistently. By chipping away at your passion and turning into a specialist in it, you will eventually have the chance to profit from it. Be prepared to grab that chance!

Pick an esteem name that impacts YOU.

A great many people would name the esteem I identified essentially as "bold". In any case, the word bold doesn't impact me. Rather the name "wind in your face" is substantially more critical for me as a basic belief.

Before settling on a choice, pursue these five stages:

Initially, survey your list of qualities. For this activity, it is best to have your qualities recorded.

At that point ask yourself this inquiry concerning the esteem you have recorded as number one: "On a size of 1 to 10, with 10 being the most astounding, how well does the apparent result of this choice or opportunity line up with esteem number one?" Then record the number.

Ask a similar inquiry regarding each an incentive on your rundown.

After you've appraised the apparent result of this choice or open door for every one of your basic beliefs, include the numbers up and locate the normal.

Lastly, assess the score. Your point is to get a score of seven or higher by and large. If you score beneath seven, the choice or opportunity may not adjust enough to your qualities to be considered.

Check in on your qualities every day
Ideally, you should "check in" on your qualities every day. (If day by day feels like too much, attempt week after week.) Personally, I do this in transit home from work. I ask myself, "How well did my choices and conduct line up with esteem #1 today?" This takes just two minutes yet furnishes you with a decent feeling of what to enhance the following day. It keeps you focused and in contact with what is imperative to you.

Recognize What's Important
Recognize what's vital for you. Record your best 5 things that you accept are the pith of how you want to live. This can incorporate things like "family time," or "sing each day." It could also incorporate increasingly complex ideas, like "genuineness" and "straightforwardness."

Discover a Way to Give Back
Accomplish something that the two distinctions your convictions and passions, while giving something back to the world. By giving something back, we definitely discover reason in the demonstration. By developing a greater amount of these exercises, you will discover your life has additionally significance and reason behind it.

Purposefully help yourself to remember your qualities
It's essential to have a visual notice of your qualities, notwithstanding your rundown of qualities. This keeps them up front in your brain. Here are some easy approaches to help yourself to remember your qualities all the time:

Make a screensaver.
Try not to belittle the intensity of a post-it.

Discover an image that speaks to one of your qualities and keep it somewhere you will see it day by day.

Pick a melody to speak to at least one of your qualities and hear it out once per day as a major aspect of your morning, evening, or night custom.

Simplify Your Life
By simplifying your life, you'll have more opportunity to do what satisfies you and gives your life meaning. It can also help decrease pressure and make your overall life easier to oversee. It can also incredibly enhance your profitability. If you've never attempted to simplify things, it really is an incredible inclination.

Find Your Life's Purpose
If you needed to give yourself a reason to live, what might it be? What might you rely on? What standards do you hold most astounding? Is your life's motivation to help other people? Is it to rouse others with incredible masterpieces, or you words? Finding your life's motivation is an overwhelming task, and when I previously heard the thought, I had no clue where to begin. For techniques on finding your life's motivation, I prescribe Steve Pavlina's blog passages regarding the matter. I also suggest perusing the article What Makes Life Worth Living.

Act naturally Aware
Know about yourself and your activities. Stay aware of what you do consistently, and ensure you are living as per your standards, your life's motivation, and what you are passionate about. Survey your activities every day, considering those that strayed from your way. Work towards revising any occurrences later on. Contemplation is an incredible tool for achieving this task. It causes us increase our mindfulness for the duration of the day.

MINIMALISM AND DECLUTTERING

Focus
Instead of chasing 3 or 4 objectives and gaining next to no ground on them, put all of your energy on a certain something. Focus. Not exclusively will you alleviate a portion of the pressure associated with endeavoring to juggle such a significant number of tasks, you will be considerably more fruitful. Attempt and adjust your objective to something you are passionate about, so that there will be an inborn drive to buckle down and do well.

People More Than Things
Regularly, we are looked with wanting to purchase material merchandise. I prescribe you consider cautiously what you purchase, and think increasingly about spending your cash on experiences with loved ones. Not exclusively will this give further significance to your life by focusing on your connections instead of material riches, but you will be a more joyful individual thus.

Live With Compassion
Both for yourself, as well as other people. Remember the accompanying statement:

"One must be compassionate to one's self before outer compassion" - Dalai Lama

For a few, compassion is the reason for life, what gives it meaning, and what prompts extreme bliss.

Set Daily Goals
In the first part of the, prior day you begin your day, make a list of 3 objectives that you find satisfying and important. Ensure they adhere to your arrangement of standards and convictions. Handle the hardest things first! Try not to make this list too long. By putting too numerous things on the rundown, you'll want to perform various tasks, which isn't great, or you'll feel overpowered, which isn't great either. By endeavoring to do less, you'll wind up accomplishing more.

Doing all of these things on the double may appear to be overwhelming, but you can pick one thing at any given moment and gradually consolidate the ideas into your life. Life is about the voyage, not the goal. Carrying on with a life of direction gives both satisfaction and importance to your adventure.

MINIMALISM AND DECLUTTERING

SIMPLICITY OF MINDFULNESS AND MEDITATION

If the basic life really is the best, at that point why so few of us want to live it? I recollect a narrative about a gathering of Mongolian migrants, and the fervor when they purchased their first TV and installed it in their yurt. From that point on, each night, they were transfixed by the TV. No more narrating around the stove, no all the more playing amusements or singing melodies. The TV currently led their recreation time, as it does in such a significant number of households around the globe.

It appears we're hard-wired to search out incitement and multifaceted nature. Truth be told it takes significant control to pick a life of effortlessness, and maybe thus, a life of genuine straightforwardness can frequently turn out to be very inflexible. The straightforward life can also lean towards being oversimplified instead of basic. To imagine there are straightforward answers for our intricate issues is usually gullible – however engaging. Short, punchy three word trademarks by our pioneers make great nightly news, and can assure the watcher the issue is being dealt with. Later we usually discover that, somewhere off camera, the 'straightforward' arrangement ended up being definitely not, and frequently caused more issues which the cutting edge is currently managing.

However huge numbers of us do long for more noteworthy effortlessness. A withdraw domain offers us the chance to simplify our lives for a couple of days by evacuating a considerable lot of the regular diversions. Rather, we focus on being available in the here and now. Contingent upon the idea of the withdraw, there might be no talking, no perusing, absolutely no browsing Facebook or messages. The structure of the withdraw clarifies where our consideration ought to be – contemplation, eating, strolling, and cleaning the washroom. Toward the finish of retreats, individuals regularly talk about a profound feeling of happiness, of feeling appreciation for basic things like the trees outside the window, the ducklings they viewed amid a break, the delicate endeavors of the cooks. After some time, if we go to standard withdraws and think each day, a portion of that happiness and appreciation tends to saturate our every day lives.

The Art of Simplicity – Straightforwardness
In a fast paced occupied existence where consistently gets immediately loaded up with movement and finishing a 'plan for the day' it's easy to disregard the straightforward delight of 'simply sitting' in contemplation and the advantages it can convey to your life. Too frequently we get focused on chasing our tails getting it done, family and different duties, contemplation at that point is a Time Out of the monotonous routine of seeking after our objectives and allows the space for stillness to develop and an opportunity to recollect the straightforwardness of simply being.

Contemplation can turn into a quest for unattainable objectives of preeminent edification or relative flawlessness but by simply sitting and simply breathing there are no more desires or needing for any splendid experience, reflection would then be able to end up the statement of straightforwardness or as Zen Master Dogen educated – simply sitting is simply the outflow of illumination without whatever else included.

Maybe this is something we have lost in our cutting edge world, the capacity to simply sit still and be content. Without attempting to accomplish something or always enhance ourselves we can allow straightforwardness to rise naturally. This is something unfamiliar to us but it blends an old notice of the delight of simply being.

I have discovered the contemplation directions from a Tibetan knowledge convention called Mahamudra probably the most significant I have ever run over and it's the effortlessness of the guidelines that is accurately its splendor. Mahamudra is discovering harmony and stillness by giving the mind a chance to be as it is without controlling it or attempting to transform anything; the consciousness of things ideal similarly as they are. Its an acknowledgment that things similarly as they are correct currently have a specific stunner to them regardless of how disordered or untidy everything may appear.

Giving the mind a chance to be similarly as it is, at that point basically sit still and essentially breath and the delight of straightforwardness and genuineness easily emerges. Without constraining anything simply unwind and see the effortlessness of being in the now. The renowned Chinese Philosopher Confucius says:

When we consider contemplation, numerous pictures ring a bell. There may even be sure stigmas associated with it. Usually saw as religion-based or as "another age" convention, with yogis roosted in the lotus position reciting Ohm for quite a long time.

In truth, there are numerous approaches to characterize reflection. But it can also be inspected from a non-denominational, target focal point. Its training doesn't need to be convoluted or grandiose. Contemplation can just be tied in with being still and quiet. It very well may focus on breath. It tends to be the specialty of quieting our brains.

"Life is really basic, but we demand making it muddled."

In the present current culture, contemplation can be a profitable tool with a large group of advantages. There is a plenitude of writing about its exceptional advantages. For example, its training has been known to alleviate pressure, stress, uneasiness and sorrow. It can help construct confidence and mindfulness. It can even battle a wide assortment of ailments. Pinto includes, "And the best part is that there are positively no unfavorable symptoms. I imagine that nowadays, we as a whole realize that a positive perspective has a solid positive effect on one's wellbeing, connections, and occupation."

To put it plainly, contemplation can enhance our lives. Our timetables are over-stuffed and we want to top off every minute. We get occupied. We fixate on the past and worry about what's to come. Contemplation recommends that when you sit in stillness, our outlook can be changed. We are established right now. From that point, we can get away from the continuous racket of our psyche and look at things in a progressively target way.

Its training can be valuable for the entire family. Reflection instructors concur that children can also receive its rewards. "Kids are naturals when it comes to thinking because they have a characteristic affinity for bliss, and for looking for their own joy," clarifies Pinto.

At the end of the day, reflection ought to be polished in a cheerful and straightforward way. If you might want to start a contemplation practice in your family, begin with the basics. The thought is to enjoy a reprieve from your bustling life and cut out some holy time. There are contemplation classes, books and recordings to rouse you. See what impacts you and consolidate that into your life. Keep a receptive outlook and see what benefits contemplation can convey to your whole family.

I think the specialty of straightforwardness is allowing things to be without control or manufacture – euphoria and harmony can be found whenever you want to stop, be still and simply take some cognizant breaths. This is the Way of reflection and figuring out how to appreciate the basic things in life is really a gift.

To have the capacity to relish some tea, appreciate gazing toward the sky or simply grinning to yourself about being alive is magnificently basic and at the some time totally fulfilling. Keeping it straightforward is keeping it genuine. Effortlessness also infers a capacity to not need to intellectually clarify each and every thing that occurs but

MINIMALISM AND DECLUTTERING

rather to acknowledge things as they are with a feeling of transparency and riddle.

It is something that must be experienced instead of discussed, and regularly to state the words 'I don't have a clue' is the start of unwinding into a honest straightforwardness. Effortlessness is constantly accessible when you set aside the opportunity to see the sheer receptiveness of the present minute.

ALEXANDRA JESSEN

30-DAY MINIMALISM

CHALLENGE

For this post, I've gathered 30 one-day assignments to enable you to plunge your toes into minimalist living, find loads of new things about yourself and get a major head begin. If you want to carry on with a more straightforward, progressively deliberate life with less stuff but additional time and energy for the general population and things you adore, make January your period of progress!

The standards for the challenge: Do one assignment consistently, the request is your call. Try not to avoid multi day. That is it.

Stay disconnected for one day
Web based life, interminable news streams and articles all deplete our energy and keep us in a steady occupied state. So today: Log off and appreciate the serenity of remaining separated.

Relinquish an objective
The way to accomplishing objectives as a minimalist is to set the correct ones in any case! Rather than chasing things you figure you should want, make sense of what might really satisfy you. Relinquish any objectives that aren't important to you for good today.

Identify your 3-6 principle needs
Most importantly, minimalism is tied in with making sense of what is important most to you in life and how to add a greater amount of that to your everyday daily schedule. Today: Dig profound and make a list of your 3-6 top needs in life.

MINIMALISM AND DECLUTTERING

Pursue a wake-up routine
Begin your day with an unwinding and empowering wake-up routine, rather than promptly browsing your email or online networking encourages. Reflect, compose, do yoga or read a book.

Streamline your perusing list
Today: Downsize your perusing list, withdraw and expel bookmarks. Keep just sources that are significant to you and that add something to your day.

Figure out how to appreciate isolation
Go through somewhere around 3 hours (ideally progressively) alone, without online networking or foundation prattle from the TV. Focus on what it feels like to be in total isolation and, if you like, record your contemplations.

Cut back your excellence gathering
Handle your magnificence items today! Compose a list of all that you use all the time from the highest point of your head (without checking your magnificence cupboards). Discard out or give everything else.

Kill notifications
Email and online life notifications make for an exceptionally responsive work process. Only for now: Turn off all notifications and check your feeds just at assigned occasions.

Assess your responsibilities
Record all of your customary responsibilities, for example enrollments, side ventures and different obligations. At that point be straightforward: Which of these do you just keep up out of commitment and which do you really appreciate or are important to you?

Characterize your objectives during the current year
Defining objectives shields you from living in a receptive, passive manner and causes you adjust your every day activities to your actual needs. Today, put aside something

like thirty minutes to choose 1-3 major, energizing objectives during the current year.

Take care of your personal business
Hold a full evening to experience your closet piece-by-piece and dispose of whatever doesn't make you feel certain and propelled. Look at this exercise manual if you have an inclination that your closet could use a patch up.

Make a stride towards taking in another expertise
Learning expands your frame of reference and can be so much fun! Today, pick an expertise you have dependably been interested about, accumulate whatever you need and begin!

Look at your day by day propensities
Today, investigate your regular propensities, from your morning schedule to the manner in which you work to your night exercises. Which propensities might you be able to enhance, which would it be advisable for you to drop, which new ones might you be able to get?

Ruminate for fifteen minutes
Contemplation diminishes pressure and nervousness and gives you a huge amount of additional energy and mental lucidity. Use an application like Headspace to try it out today.

Declutter your computerized life
Deal with your advanced clutter today: Spring-clean your work area, erase any documents you needn't bother with any longer and set up a basic, simple envelope structure.

No-objection day
Griping is never beneficial and an impetus for negative idea designs. Challenge yourself to not gripe about small stuff today. Either acknowledge the circumstance and proceed onward, or discover an answer.

No email or web based life until lunch
Use your most profitable hours of the day to complete poo and oppose checking your feeds until the point when

noon. At that point commend the amount more you achieved!

Try not to purchase anything for 24 hours
Leap forward an undesirable cycle of emotional spending by going on a one-day shopping fast. Try not to purchase anything, not in any case nourishment or basics, for 24 hours (ensure you prepare ahead of time). At that point perceive how you feel!

Practice single-tasking
Nothing channels energy faster than always exchanging between numerous tasks. Practice really focusing on one thing at any given moment utilizing a clock like this one. Stick to short blasts of concentrated work with standard breaks in the middle.

Unfollow and unfriend
De-stretch your web based life experience by being somewhat more specific about who you pursue. Do you really need to remain Facebook companions with people you haven't addressed in years? Experience your list and scale down.

Go for a walk and practice care
Strolls are an incredible chance to rehearse care. Pick a recognizable course and give careful consideration to your surroundings with all detects. You'll be astonished what number of new things you'll notice and how invigorated you'll feel after.

No TV all day, read
All electronic gadgets emanate a blue light that irritates our melatonin generation and decreases rest quality. Along these lines, rather than completion your night with a few scenes of your most loved show, snuggle up on the lounge chair with a decent book today!

Diary for twenty minutes
Composing causes you arrange your contemplations and de-stresses. Take a seat for twenty minutes today to

expound on whatever rings a bell. If you like it, consider consolidating a speedy day by day composing session into your customary everyday practice.

Make a loosening up sleep time schedule

Enhance your rest quality and energy levels by setting aside the opportunity to legitimately slow down toward the finish of every day. Do some composition, read a decent book, have some tea, prepare everything for the following day, and so forth. Attempt it today!

Go unabashed

Re-set what you consider fundamental by following a stripped down magnificence routine only for now (no make up and negligible healthy skin). You may well find that huge numbers of the items you thought you need are really discretionary and would then be able to streamline your standard schedule a bit.

Practice appreciation

Turning into a minimalist is most importantly about being careful and valuing the little (and huge) things that are now a piece of your life. Assignment for now: Write a not insignificant rundown of everything (and everybody) you are appreciative for in life.

Leave an entire day impromptu

In our way of life, we are so used to making the most out of each free moment of the day, it very well may be relatively unnerving to not have any plans for once. Be bold today and see where it takes you.

Identify your pressure triggers

The initial move towards lessening regular pressure is to pinpoint your own triggers. Attempt this: Take notes of your feelings of anxiety and your exercises at normal interims all through a weekday. When you have identified your pressure triggers, make sense of how you could avert or balance them later on.

MINIMALISM AND DECLUTTERING

Get out your garbage cabinet

Disposing of clutter can have a relatively remedial impact, because it encourages you manage all of the different emotions that are appended to your stuff. Finish your own treatment session today by clearing out the most cluttered cabinet/box/corner of your house.

Assess your last five purchases

Growing progressively moral and less consumerist ways of managing money is critical to carrying on with a less difficult life. Today, assess your last five trivial purchases. How useful did they end up being and how might you enhance your purchasing choices later on?

ALEXANDRA JESSEN

TIPS TO DECLUTTER YOUR HOME

When you've managed the emotional reasons you can begin to get breaking! Here's 10 tips for decluttering:

Use a 'maybes' heap.
Rather than obsessing about a few things, have a 'maybes' heap and come back to it later and manage them all in one go.

Work rapidly
don't spend an excessively long time umming and ahhing over what to keep. Your gut drive is usually right. If in uncertainty – ask yourself when you 'genuineness' last used the thing – if it's more than 1 season back then receptacle it!

Pass on the pleasure.
If something has given you pleasure in the past but you believe you most likely won't use it again – pass on that pleasure. Envision how incredible it will be to give that experience to another person.

Discover 'places' for things.
Settle on a place for things like your keys, sunglasses or wallet. Stick to it and you'll never lose another thing again!

Try not to consider it too important!
Try not to think about this as a major errand rather choose to have some good times with it. Wrench up the stereo with your most loved tunes and chime in while you declutter.

Help other people less blessed than you.
Consider decluttering a beneficent demonstration. You can give away things that you never again need to the

individuals who truly are in need. When we take the focus off ourselves and onto others it prevents us from fixating on insignificant things.

Sort things into 4 expansive heaps
the primary area to toss out, the second segment for philanthropy, the third segment to offer and the fourth segment to keep.

Set yourself an objective or a due date.
Defining objectives makes inspiration and energy so you can dedicate yourself completely to the task. If you need some assistance with defining objectives read 8 Tips for defining objectives.

Focus on the result.
Picture how stunning your home will look when you're set. Have a reasonable picture of what you want it to resemble – and continue alluding back to this to prop you up!

ALEXANDRA JESSEN

DECLUTTERING: PRACTICAL STEPS FOR LIVING WITH LESS

Begin easy. "Your initial phase the correct way does not need to be a major one. Our own adventure started by expelling the clutter from our vehicles. Literally. The primary things we limited were ketchup parcels, Happy Meal toys, old receipts, and seldom used music CDs. It wasn't huge, but it made us move the correct way.

"Our next tasks incorporated the family room, the room, and our closet. Each room or storage room was somewhat harder than the past. But we found vital force in the early strides to help bring us through the difficult ones not far off," Becker said.

Pick a lived-in region to start. "When you initially start to declutter your home, pick a zone that is frequently used. There are numerous advantages to owning less - clear, open spaces with less diversions is truly outstanding. As you evacuate clutter, you will rapidly experience them.

"And the most ideal approach to completely understand these advantages is to start decluttering a room that is used frequently. This could be a family room, a room, an office, or a restroom. Begin decluttering in an easy, lived-in zone. You'll cherish it. And find increased inspiration," Becker said.

Contact each thing. "Your decluttering venture isn't a race. It took a very long time to aggregate all the clutter in your home and it will take in excess of an evening or end of the week to evacuate it. My very own group of four took nine months. You will love taking as much time as is needed. And you will love requiring the additional push to physically contact each thing in your home.

MINIMALISM AND DECLUTTERING

"Physically handling every thing powers our brains to settle on purposeful choices about them. In the wake of contacting every thing, put it in one of three heaps: keep, migrate, or expel. From that point, handle quickly. And then rehash," Becker said.

Incline toward giving over moving. "You can make more cash by moving your unneeded clutter. And if you really need the cash, take the plunge. There are endless sites that can help. But know that endeavoring to move your clutter is tedious, bulky, and regularly adds to the worry of decluttering.

"If cash isn't a prompt worry for your family, move your significant things on Ebay, but give everything else to a nearby philanthropy. You will discover delight and satisfaction in liberality - and that experience will be imperative going ahead as you try to conquer the device of commercialization," Becker said.

Peruse a book. "The primary book I read on decluttering was Clear Your Clutter with Feng Shui by Karen Kingston. While feng shui never turned into a core value in my home, the musings in the book were useful for our adventure. It is essential to be reminded that others battle with a similar issue. And it is gainful to hear new answers for these issues.

"The book was great, regardless I suggest it. But I also prescribe Simplify, Organised Simplicity, The Joy of Less, and The Life-Changing Magic of Tidying Up. Any of them will be useful and persuading," Becker said.

Tell a companion. "Satisfaction is most satisfying when it is imparted to other people. Recount your anecdote about your goals to declutter. You will discover individuals are eager to attempt it themselves. They will support you. They will rouse you by considering you responsible and ask you how things are going whenever you see them.

"As an extra advantage, when you share your story, you will be helped again to remember the reasons you chose to declutter in any case," Becker said.

Approve of blemish. "Try not to give ideal a chance to wind up the adversary of better. The first occasion when you experience your home, you won't expel all the clutter. You'll keep stuff that didn't need to be kept. You'll see it too difficult to part with a few things. You may even evacuate some things you'll finish up wishing you had kept," Becker said.

MINIMALISM AND DECLUTTERING

TECHNIQUES FOR PRACTICAL DECLUTTERING

There isn't one right approach to declutter, but much of the time, the dispose of everything medium-term strategy isn't practical. Consider the enormous changes you've made in your life.

Play the memory diversion.
If you keep things away, you've likely composed the substance outwardly of each crate. Something else, how might you realize what was inside? Recollecting what's in the crate without a mark is a genuine trial of how vital the stuff is to you. Fill a crate with things you aren't exactly prepared to part with, but aren't sure you really need. Stamp the case "give following 30 days." Then move the case outside of anyone's ability to see, marked. "Give if I needn't bother with." After 30 days, if you can't recollect what's in the crate or don't miss the substance, give it all without opening.

Welcome everybody to the gathering.
When you start decluttering, welcome your family to participate. Try not to drive, welcome. Keep in mind, however, that while the easiest place to search for clutter is in another person's space, your family may dislike the weight. Along these lines, begin with your very own things. Give relatives a chance to take a shot at decluttering their own things at their very own pace. If you want people to see the delight in less, live happily with less yourself.

Set the stage.
Challenge yourself and your family to three months of just purchasing the basics and/or disposing of something whenever another thing comes into your home. Approaching things incorporate purchases, gifts, and items from school or

the workplace. At the end of the day, everything checks. If you purchase another match of shoes, give an old combine. If you purchase another restorative item, hurl the leftovers of old ones that are presumably terminated at any rate. If you purchase new wine glasses, give the ones you were utilizing previously. This will help anticipate clutter creep while you are decluttering.

Obviously characterize the mission.
There is a major difference among arranging and decluttering. Sorting out methods you're simply moving stuff starting with one place then onto the next. Rather than buckling down to locate the ideal spot for something, perceive that it probably won't have a place in your home or your heart at all any longer.

Declutter In Stages.
Begin with the easy stuff to construct your decluttering muscles. Things, for example, copies, embellishing things, kitchen hardware you haven't used in years, things you don't use or appreciate, and things away that haven't been a piece of your life for quite a while will be easier to release. Every thing you let go of will give you the quality and inspiration to relinquish the following.

Excursion Light.
Apply your decluttering procedures when you travel, and help up your suitcase. Pressing softly is an incredible practice for living delicately. On your next trek, pack for a large portion of the length of your get-away. Leave the "to be safe" things at home, and notice how light you feel when strolling through the air terminal, unloading at the inn, and investigating another area without stressing over all of your stuff.

Relinquish your emotions too.
When you let go of things that you've clutched because you spent too much cash to get them or influenced a significant venture on them, to endeavor to also relinquish the blame of terrible purchasing choices and overspending.

MINIMALISM AND DECLUTTERING

If you battle with blame about giving up, hanging tight, cash spent, or time wasted, it's an ideal opportunity to shift each liable idea to one of appreciation. If you are considering, "I shouldn't have spent that cash," exchange your idea for "I'm appreciative that I perceive what's most essential to me now."

You have effectively sufficiently paid. If you don't relinquish the blame, you will keep on paying with your time, consideration, energy, and heart. The genuine expense of the things you are holding is a lot higher than the numbers on the sticker price.

Ask For Help.

Some of the time, we are so connected to our stuff that it's difficult to realize when to hang on and when to give up. Ask a companion or relative to encourage you. Give this individual a chance to cast a ballot "yes" or "no" to dress, beautiful pieces, and different things. Far and away superior, swap administrations, and consent to go to your companion's home beside respond.

Reconsider wistfulness.

The last phase of decluttering is usually put something aside for the all the more challenging things, including the costly and nostalgic stuff. If the costly things have no significance or reason in your life, move them, and use the returns to settle debt or give to philanthropy.

If you are sparing things to pass down to your youngsters, think about that they most likely don't want it. A Washington Post article called "Stuff it: Millennials Nix their Parent's Treasures" paints a convincing picture for guardians who are hanging on: "As people born after WW2, conceived somewhere in the range of 1946 and 1964, begin wiping out upper rooms and basements, many are finding that twenty to thirty year olds, conceived somewhere in the range of 1980 and 2000, are not all that keen on the lifestyle trappings or nostalgic memorabilia they were so affectionately raised with. Scaling back specialists and expert coordinators are encouraging guardians whose youngsters seem to have lost any wistful connection to their lovable child shoes and family treasure quilts." at the end of the day, your child's don't want your stuff, so you can relinquish it now.

Your kids realize genuine treasures are not in the loft or contained in any physical thing.

Account for additional.
Decluttering starts when you want less; less clutter, less debt, and less diversions, but eventually, you'll begin to want more. Prepare for a greater amount of what you really want from your life, space for how you want to contribute to the world, and space for what makes a difference to your heart. Account for a greater amount of the well done.

Each of these gradual systems for handy decluttering will enable you to make more space, time, and love effortlessly rather than battle, and bliss rather than despair. Be thoughtful to yourself and to your family as you figure out how to relinquish the clutter, and clutch the affection.

HOW TO START DECLUTTERING YOUR LIFE:

5 SIMPLE STEPS

How to Declutter

"It's anything but an every day increase, but a day by day decrease. Hack away at the inessentials."

Bruce Lee

I cherish decluttering.

Why?

Because a life with less clutter makes it easier to:

Lessen the day by day stress and find inward harmony.

Focus and to complete a superior occupation (and frequently do it snappier too).

Keep your consideration consistently on what is most imperative and important in life.

Clutter makes diversion. It can make pressure and disarray that you may not know that it's making.

But after you have decluttered there is usually a vibe of feeling more quiet and lighter, more cheery and having the capacity to think all the more plainly.

Decluttering a cabinet, rack or some sort of room in your life can be a surprisingly positive experience not simply practically. But for you as an individual both emotionally and mentally.

This is the most imperative reason why I declutter.

But it, obviously, also opens up space. It can push you to at times procure a touch of additional cash. It can make another person more joyful by giving them something you have no use for any longer.

If you have only 5 or 10 minutes to save today and want to venture out simplify your external and internal life then I suggest uncluttering only one small space in your house.

Here's the manner by which I declutter in five speedy advances.

Pick a cabinet or a rack. Void it out and get it out. Put everything that was in that space in one major heap.

Settle on decisions about those things, each one in turn. For every thing in that heap ask yourself this: have I used this in the past year? If not, at that point usually quite safe to state that you won't use it later on either.

Give it away or trash it? If you are not keeping it then you might want to offer it to somebody you realize that you think could make great use of it. Or then again you can give it away to your neighborhood philanthropy. If that is the case placed it in a crate or sack for that reason. And if you simply want to trash it then put it at that point place it in a sack where you'll gather the trash things amid this brief uncluttering session.

If you are keeping it, at that point locate a home for it. It could be at one of the front corners of your cabinet or to one side in the best retire of your bookcase. Having a home for every thing where you set it back each time subsequent to utilizing it will diminish the week by week clutter in your home and you will dependably have the capacity to easily discover the thing.

If you are uncertain about the thing at that point place it in a 6-month box. Put that case away somewhere where you can easily get to it – a wardrobe for instance – if you need

MINIMALISM AND DECLUTTERING

something from it. Outwardly of the container compose the date when you put the stuff in it. a half year later get the case and see what is still in it. If you haven't used those things in the past a half year then you have no need for them and you can securely give them away or toss them out.

By making small 5-10 minute strides when you have some an opportunity to save you can declutter a ton over fourteen days.

Or then again that first small advance may lead you to uncluttering an entire room without a moment's delay. Or on the other hand rouse you to take 5-10 minutes tomorrow to begin decluttering your work space.

ALEXANDRA JESSEN

HERE'S HOW TO MAKE MINIMALISM WORK FOR YOU

It's likely not a stretch to state that you have a ton of stuff you needn't bother with. Regardless of whether you endeavor to remain over clutter and you're truly great at keeping everything perfect and clean, you could stand to scale it back a bit – everybody could. But we've all turned out to be so used to amassing things and utilizing them as a measure of our prosperity, that disposing of all that appears to be a stage in reverse. However, minimalists have figured out how to do only that.

The minimalism lifestyle has been picking up steam throughout the previous couple of years and it is by all accounts achieving a point where the vast majority in any event think about it. Why? Because it's sort of fascinating to perceive how people who live in modest houses figure out how to benefit as much as possible from each and every inch of room or how liberating it is to live with less.

There are a lot of books on minimalism if you're keen on perusing up on it, but probably the best ones incorporate The Life-Changing Magic of Tidying Up: The Japanese Art of Decluttering and Organizing by Maria Kondo, Minimalism: Live a Meaningful Life by Joshua Fields Millburn, The Joy of Less by Francine Jay and Everything That Remains: A Memoir by the Minimalists by Joshua Fields Millburn and Ryan Nicodemus. All four present the masters of carrying on with a life less confused by things and all the more loaded with experiences. Or on the other hand you could simply watch the narrative on Netflix!

You might not want to go to boundaries to wind up a genuine minimalist, but that doesn't mean there aren't some minimalist standards you can't matter to your life to some degree. It's all about parity. Here are a couple of ways you can consolidate minimalism into your life without surrendering all that you possess.

Begin small

Discarding or giving all that you possess in one day isn't likely to be an extraordinary thought. Rather, you need to begin with one zone of your home, like your kitchen for instance. Do you have a group of old dishes that you never use but you're keeping on hand "in the event of some unforeseen issue"? Possibly it's an ideal opportunity to give them away. Because it's not useful to you any longer doesn't mean another person won't esteem it.

Hastily discarding everything is anything but a genuine answer for your clutter issue. You must be attentive and deliberate about what you want to keep and what you want to dispose of, or else you won't bring an end to any negative behavior patterns and you'll simply supplant it all with new stuff. To begin, attempt the 30 Day Minimalism Game

Dark colored Wooden Book Shelf

If you took a gander at your closet truly, what level of the apparel you claim would you say you have worn in the last 3 months? Shouldn't something be said about the last a half year, or the last year? If you have things that never wear, for what reason would you say you are keeping them? It's another case of accumulating things "in the event that something goes wrong" you may need them one day. But the thing is, you wouldn't wear that dark dress again because you either don't love it any longer or it doesn't fit, which is the reason you've just worn it once at any rate.

It may sound amusing, but the less garments you have, the less time you'll spend griping that you don't have anything to wear. Keep your closet basic and you'll never have an issue assembling an outfit, last moment or not.

Pinpoint the things that satisfy you

Being a minimalist isn't about just having things that are significant. You can and ought to have a couple of things that really fulfill you regardless of whether they aren't really down to earth. If you want to peruse, it's alright to have a book gathering. If music is your passion, don't dispose of your phonograph and guitar because you don't use them consistently. You're ought to have assets that really speak to your identity as long as they bring you joy. The key is to know precisely what fulfills you so you're OK with letting everything else go.

Investigate your ways of managing money

What you burn through cash on is a decent marker of what you consider "necessities". Do you go out to eat a great deal? It is safe to say that you are an impulsive customer who purchases things that are at a bargain regardless of whether you needn't bother with them? Do you adhere to a financial plan, or simply spend and seek after the best? Limit the vulnerability in your spending and you'll finish up with less random purchases that you don't actually need. If you find that you frequently purchase things as an approach to perk yourself up, it may be an ideal opportunity to locate another approach to diminish pressure.

CONCLUSION

Minimalism has become a popular word in the last 10 years but it is so much more than that. As consumerism takes a choke hold over people, some have chosen to take a step back and see what really matters in their lives.

Minimalism is about remaining happy and content while having less. We will show you how other people have walked away from the hype of consumerism.

The prospect of living with less clutter is speaking to many, and the advantages are outstanding. Owning less stuff implies possessing more energy for the most essential aspects of our lives, and even feeling progressively good in our own home. As alluring as those outcomes might be, the prospect of decluttering a home can be overpowering with a lifetime of stuff gathered in basements and storage rooms.

While limiting will likely require significant time and exertion, having a decent decluttering strategy to pursue can have a significant effect.

It wasn't until Amy and I discovered a decluttering strategy called The Minimalist Game that we began gaining predictable ground towards disposing of the clutter in our lives.

Whichever decluttering strategy you pick, it's most essential that you just begin. Life improves past the consistent worry of clutter, it just takes some time and exertion to arrive.

Life is intended to be experienced, not passively anticipated through the screens that encompass us once a day. It may sound threatening, but there are really just a couple general ideas you need to keep mind. So whether you're keen on exchanging your marketed lifestyle for finish straightforwardness, executing a few tips to help you serenely live with less, or just decluttering your condition for increased association and decreased pressure, these small tips will undoubtedly set you on course for progress - all without making too much disturbance your day by day schedule.

Simply ahead and begin living spotless, light and free, no bargains!

Minimalism will appear to be unique for everybody, and it doesn't mean you can't have a house, vehicle or occupation.

It's tied in with decluttering yourself from material belongings and freeing your life of stays.

Minimalism is the tool that allows you to focus on just the vital things. It allows you to carry on with your life all the more intentionally and with significance.

Minimalism is a lifestyle, it's a voyage that takes every day focus and duty to enhancement. Making small, day by day upgrades is critical.

I hope this book was able to help you to get clear idea about minimalism & decluttering. Thanks for reading the book.

www.ingramcontent.com/pod-product-compliance
Lightning Source LLC
Chambersburg PA
CBHW081153070526
44583CB00021B/2817